COLLEGE 101

Making the Most of Your Freshman Year

Revised Edition

Ronald T. Farrar

Peterson's Guides
Princeton, New Jersey

**Library of Congress Cataloging-in-Publication
Data**

Farrar, Ronald T.
      College 101 : making the most of your
   freshman year / Ronald T. Farrar. — Rev. ed.
         p.   cm.
      ISBN 0-87866-730-X (pbk.)
      1. College student orientation—United
States. 2. College freshmen—United States.
I. Title. II. Title: College one hundred one.
III. Title: College one hundred and one.
LB2343.32.F37   1988   88-25955
378'.198—dc19   CIP

Printed in the United States of America

10 9 8 7 6 5 4 3 2 1

for
Gayla Dennis Farrar

ACKNOWLEDGMENTS

A number of persons helped with this book and should be thanked. First are the students, faculty members, and staff colleagues with whom I've worked over the years. Their advice, encouragement, and examples are reflected throughout these pages. I am specifically grateful to Dr. Louise Dutt in the Counseling Office and George Dexter in Admissions at the University of Kentucky, along with financial aid officers, housing administrators, reference librarians, and—especially—faculty members and students of the School of Journalism. A thoughtful study of the freshman year, given direction by Dr. Robert Zumwinkle and largely written by Dr. John B. Stephenson, now president of Berea College, was most helpful. These individuals and their counterparts on other campuses provided invaluable assistance and I am grateful. At the University of South Carolina, I am especially indebted to Robert P. Godfrey and Denise A. Wellman in Student Financial Aid and Dr. Judith H. Small in Counseling, among many other colleagues. Van Kornegay and Craig Paddock, one a computer whiz, the other an indefatigable graduate assistant, solved numerous technical problems associated with the word processing of this revised edition.

Through the teaching, research, and service of Dr. John N. Gardner and Professor Jerome Jewler, the University of South Carolina has become internationally acclaimed for its leadership in the study of the freshman year. Many colleges and universities in the United States and abroad have benefited from their efforts, which, though not related to this book, nevertheless deserve special mention. Certainly they have created a campus climate in which freshman achievement and retention command a deservedly high priority.

Several organizations generously granted permission to quote from their publications: Utah State University and Gordon College; M. Evans and Company, the publishers of *Aerobics,* written by Dr. Kenneth H. Cooper; and the editors of the *Bulletin of Yale University* (series 78, number 6), the *School Musician,* and the *University of Iowa Spectator.* Both the Lexington Rape Crisis Center and the Kentucky Alcoholism Council provided responses to specific inquiries. There are of course others who have contributed directly or indirectly over the years—so many, in fact, that it's not possible to name them. Needless to say, however, any errors that might appear in these pages are not their doing, but mine alone.

Thanks, too, to my editors at Peterson's Guides: Christopher Billy, who worked long and hard developing the original edition some years ago, and Andrea E. Lehman, who handled the revision.

Finally, I want to acknowledge three debts that are as important as they are personal: One is to the memory of my late parents, Truman and Grace Farrar, who at no small sacrifice to themselves supported my own journey through undergraduate days a generation ago. Second, to my daughter, Janet Farrar Worthington, and son, Bradley T. Farrar, whose college experiences, some of them, and good counsel are reflected in the tone and content throughout this book. The third, and clearly most impossible debt to repay, is to my wife, Gayla Dennis Farrar, to whom this work and all it represents is dedicated.

—RTF

CONTENTS

INTRODUCTION

This book has but one subject—college—and one premise: The more you know about college ahead of time, the easier your adjustment will be.

In these pages you'll find answers to well over 100 questions about life at college—questions dealing with courses and professors, money matters, socializing, making the most of time, and ways to find help when you need it. These are the questions that students—and their parents—most often ask. I don't claim to know all the answers myself (and beware of any individual who does), but I have learned where to look to find information that can help, and I can point you in the right direction.

Each college student is different—heaven help any professor who forgets this—but freshmen everywhere tend to encounter many of the same kinds of difficulties. Whether you're off to a private school, a state university, or a community college, you'll run into some of the same emotional jolts and be required to undergo many of the same adjustments as your fellow freshmen everywhere.

This book is *not* your personal flight plan through college. A flight plan sets forth highly specific routings, and no deviations are allowed. The college experience and your own personality are much too subtle and complex for that. What you'll find here instead is a compilation of concerns other students have faced, along with advice and some ideas about how to deal with them.

Abraham Lincoln once observed that "nobody ever got lost on a straight road." The route through college is one of the best journeys you'll ever make, but it is a circuitous, sometimes confusing, and occasionally frustrating road to travel. This book is designed to alert you to the hairpin turns and to the places where avalanches occur and to help you over a rough spot or two along the way.

CHAPTER 1

SETTLING IN

Q What should I pack?

A The overpowering tendency is to take too much—more clothes, appliances, trinkets, and other assorted gear than can be comfortably kept in your tiny half of a residence hall room. Even so, there are a number of items you'll need for campus survival.

For your desk: Scissors, tape (clear and masking), paper clips, a small stapler and a supply of staples, ballpoint pens, pencils, lots of paper, a highlighter for underlining key passages in your books, a few bottles of white-out to cover your writing mistakes, stationery, envelopes, and plenty of stamps. Several small note pads for phone messages and an address book are also useful.

For studying: A good dictionary is an absolute must. Also essential are a thesaurus, for those times when your vocabulary fails you, and a scholarly style manual showing correct form for footnotes and bibliography. You might want to bring along one or two exceptionally well-written papers from your high school days; you can use the format and outline for guidance in case your skills need some brushing-up.

For maintenance: Shoe polish, a sewing kit with lots of safety pins for quick repairs, straight pins, needles, and thread in various shades.

Laundry paraphernalia: Detergent, liquid soap for hand washables, and clothespins. A laundry basket, though bulky, can double as a container for other items as well, and is especially useful when you're moving in and out and carting around loose gear. You may prefer a laundry bag, which holds just as much and can be stored much more easily.

Appliances: An iron. Some dorms furnish a communal iron and ironing board; you can't count on the reliability of these irons, though, and you may not want to wait in line. Also a hot pot. You'll crave food at odd hours, especially when you're studying late, and you may not want to leave your room to get it. Include several cans of soup and a pan of some sort for making emergency meals if you run out of money or miss the cafeteria's closing time. At least one good lamp will improve the looks of things and spare you from having to endure the glare that dormitory ceiling lights can cause. Better pack an extension cord as well.

Shower gear: A bucket or plastic tray for shampoo, soap, toothpaste, and other toiletries. Also shower thongs (athlete's foot is, unfortunately, a common malady in residence halls) and a robe to wear as you travel between

5

your room and the shower. A large beach towel will serve equally well, especially if you attach a strip of Velcro along the edges to make the towel hold fast by itself, leaving your hands free.

For storage: Shoeboxes or a hanging shoe rack. It's not easy to store shoes in dorm rooms. Though they may be more trouble, the boxes are neater, and you'll probably also save time by being able to locate your shoes when you need them. *Note well:* Label one shoebox *Important Business* and use it for storing receipts, cancelled checks, housing contract, schedule cards, and so on.

For the walls: At least two posters and several small photographs. The photos may make you a tad homesick, but they make fine conversation starters when your neighbors are visiting. A bulletin or memo board, for messages and notes, is essential.

Medical supplies: Headache remedies, cold and cough medicines, adhesive bandages, antiseptic spray. Also cotton balls, tissues, and cotton swabs. Remember: Dorm rooms don't come equipped with things that your mom, the miracle worker, could always produce when you needed them.

Linens: Two sets of sheets, pillowcases, towels, and washcloths. You may have great intentions, but it's likely you won't do laundry until it's absolutely necessary.

And various other items, including

- Your high school yearbook. Believe it or not, you *will* want to look at it.
- A wastebasket. Even if your room already has one, you can use another.
- An umbrella. At least one, and you might want to bring a spare. I've had students complain that their umbrellas were stolen from under their chairs during a class. Desperate weather brings on desperate behavior. Also, high winds can cause umbrellas to crumple; on many high-rise campuses there are literally wind tunnels, areas between buildings where the wind crashes through with enough force to power Holland.
- An alarm clock, the old-fashioned kind that sounds an alarm that will wake the dead. (Windup clocks are more reliable; if there are power failures your electric clock will fail you.)
- Dishes: at least one plate, a bowl, two glasses, spoons, knives, and forks.
- Your old pillow. You'll need the comfort and security of your favorite, plumped-just-right pillow. Besides, some institutional pillows are rocks.
- A small TV set, probably, and a radio, most definitely.
- At least two crates. These can hold anything from books to sweaters and may serve as shelves and bedside tables.

If you're moving into an apartment instead of a dorm room, you'll need additional housekeeping gear as well. Your folks can help you with the specifics, but make sure these are on your list: a small tool kit, which you can use to install, among other things, a smoke detector.

You'll be tempted to delay buying clothes until you reach the campus so you can be certain of getting the "in" styles. Two points, however, should be borne in mind: (1) The shops near most campuses tend to be pretty pricey, and (2) if you buy your clothes at school, you may have to pay for them with your own spending money, whereas if you buy your clothes before you leave home, your parents are likely to foot the bill. Your own budget meter isn't apt to start running until after you arrive at school. In other words, if your parents buy now, you won't have to pay later.

Q How are roommates assigned?

A The roommate, as a thoughtful writer, Constance L. Hays, put it in a *New York Times* essay, "is at once the most keenly anticipated and deeply feared aspect of the freshman collegiate experience."

No wonder. You are about to move into a tiny cubicle of a room where you will actually *live* for the next nine months of your life—live with a person you may never have seen before. A person selected *for* you by a housing office executive or maybe an impersonal computer. What if his socks are so rank they can stand alone, and every night he props them (with feet inside) on the end of your bed as he watches TV? What if he listens only to hard rock music while you're offended by any recording that isn't country and western?

Obviously some adjustments may be in order—and that's not necessarily bad.

Some colleges and universities go to considerable lengths in an attempt to minimize the sources of potential conflict. At Duke, for example, all incoming freshmen must complete an extensive questionnaire providing information about majors, extracurricular interests, sports, entertainment, musical preferences, and so on. Many institutions also attempt to develop life-style profiles, asking entering freshmen to place themselves on a scale in such areas as:

I consider myself:

        Neat ___ ___ ___ ___ Messy

I function best:

        Early morning ___ ___ ___ Late at night

And so on. At Harvard and some other institutions as well, the parents of entering freshmen are asked to write a candid, confidential letter explaining in some detail their child's personality. The freshman, who may see himself or herself differently, is given a separate questionnaire. Other schools, such as Stanford, place a heavy emphasis on course schedules in assigning roommates on the theory that common intellectual interests will stimulate lively discussions at the dining tables and in the dorm rooms.

Other colleges and universities—including perhaps a majority of the larger state institutions—follow a pattern of random assignment. That is, they take a very few factors into account, and once that is done they simply put 2 students together (or 3 or 4, depending on the arrangement) and let nature take its course.

Even on random assignment campuses, however, at least a couple of questions are asked:

- Do you prefer a roommate who does not smoke? The tobacco issue seems to pose the most common threat to domestic peace and tranquility inside the dorm room.
- Do you have a preferred roommate? If so (and if the preference is mutual), the institution will usually attempt to pair you up.

You may be given other choices about your housing. They might include location (a matter of some importance, especially on those sprawling multiversity campuses) and costs. The typical college or university may have anything from creaking (and drafty) but elegant antebellum residence houses to modern high rises, with equally varied rental rates. So you may have some choice in these areas.

Beyond that, there's a good chance your roomie will be assigned more or less at random.

And the irony is that random assignment seems to work about as well—in terms of percentages of roommate changes that have to be dealt with—as the careful pre-enrollment screening process.

"We look upon random assignment as a positive thing," one housing director told me. "There probably won't be much screening done for you in the real world ahead. Getting to know a new roommate is a good opportunity for practice in learning to adjust, to get along."

Besides, he argued, it would be almost impossible to develop any kind of questionnaire so comprehensive as to identify all of the personality characteristics necessary to assure a perfect match of roommates.

So there you are. Much will depend, of course, on the attitudes you bring into the relationship: your willingness to listen, to be courteous and considerate, to share.

If you're really worried about your ability to adjust to your new situation, you might find useful "The Roommate Starter Kit," an inexpensive booklet that offers new roomies a format for discussing their likes and dislikes, their emotional styles, and their preliminary reactions to each other. Information about "The Roommate Starter Kit" can be obtained by writing RSK, P.O. Box 973, State College, Pennsylvania 16801.

In any event, you will be influenced by your roommate, and your adjustment to college life will, to at least some degree, be connected to the relationship you develop with your roomie. But your roommate is probably just as concerned as you are, and that's why most roommate assignments, whether done at random or not, ultimately seem to work.

Q What can I do to reduce (or prevent) the friction that might develop between my roommate and me?

A **Space.** Nothing will place a strain on your relationship quite like smashing your big toe in the middle of the night against the set of barbells your roomie forgot to put away. Or *always* having to remove her hair dryer and curling iron before you can plug in your hot pot. Come to an agreement with your roommate as to which territory is whose, and be considerate in the space you share.

Borrowing. The best policy: Don't. Before you even get to know each other very well, lay out some ground rules. Explain that from all you've heard (and read) misunderstandings and grief are avoided if you just don't borrow each other's possessions. Or, failing that, make clear which ones are *absolutely* off limits. You can do this in a diplomatic way and without being stingy or obnoxious by explaining that you know he or she must feel the same way about a favorite sweater or pair of shoes. This especially applies to car borrowing. Although on many campuses freshmen are not allowed to have cars, the problem might come up anyway. Borrowing someone else's car can cause horrendous problems—everything from a collision (with another driver, who's not insured), to your own insurance liability (your family's policy may not apply to your use of a borrowed vehicle), to your managing to get the seat stuck permanently in a position where your roommate (who is 8 inches shorter) can't reach the floor pedals, to disagreements as to how much gas the borrower used but did not replenish. As Shakespeare put it, "Neither a borrower, nor a lender be; for loan oft loses both itself *and* friend."

Responsibility. Assuming your share of it ranges all the way from *always* remembering to lock the door to your room when leaving to taking and relaying messages accurately and promptly when your roommate is out. It also includes your doing your share when it's time to clean up the place or resupply the refrigerator stock. Nothing is more infuriating than to plan ahead for that little reward before bedtime (for studying diligently for 3 hours) only to find it gone when you open the refrigerator door.

In the dorms, there's no one around who'll take responsibility for rolling you out of bed in the morning for breakfast and classes, for reminding you gently late at night to turn out the lights and go to sleep, or for regulating the volume on your bedside radio. You'll have plenty of freedom, which is nice, but your roommate and others on your floor have some freedoms too, such as the freedom not to have to endure the ear-splitting sounds of your stereo at 2:30 a.m.

Sensitivity. Maybe your roommate has had a rotten day and needs a little quiet time alone. If you can't leave the room, maybe just no conversation for a while will do. It can be nerve frazzling when someone is trying to sort things out or just needs a retreat from the pressures, momentarily, to have to endure incessant rattling about everything under the sun. Enough already! In addition to physical space, folks need mental space once in a while. That same sensitivity should dictate your behavior regarding such other potentially explosive issues as when the overhead light, the TV set, the radio, or the stereo are muted for the evening.

Being considerate of each other's needs and moods is probably the answer; if you can do that, most of the other problems will evaporate.

Q I'm basically shy. Should I worry about getting along in the dorm?

A Not at all. Remember, you won't be the only one feeling a little uneasy about moving into a new room with a total stranger. Picture this scenario: There you are—you and all your earthly goods—and not only do you not know your roommate, you also don't know the dozens of people lugging stereos and suitcases up the stairs and creating general confusion outside your strange new room. Sounds dreadful, doesn't it? But all that will soon change, and if you smile a lot, as you would if you were a foreigner in a country whose language you didn't speak, you'll be okay.

Make an effort, early on, to get acquainted. Don't hole up in your room and wait for people to drop in and introduce themselves. They might not. It's far easier to meet people when *everyone* is new during those first few days of the school year. If you hold off until patterns and relationships have already begun to form, you may find things more difficult.

Ask questions, even when you think you already know the answers: "What's the best time to do laundry?" or "What should I wear to the orientation party?" or "Should I try to get Professor Weatherbee for English 101?"

This isn't being phony; it's getting a second opinion and breaking the ice with your new neighbors.

For those who want it (and for those who don't!) dorm life itself fosters a kind of togetherness. Each floor has its community meeting places: the john, lounge, refreshment center, TV room, or laundry room. At most schools, an upperclass student or two will be on hand to arrange floor meetings, recruit for intramurals, and initiate a variety of other projects designed to encourage participation and a sense of community. These carefully chosen students are sometimes known as resident advisers or counselors, and a big part of their job is to help dorm students become acclimated to college life. Thousands of entering freshmen would describe themselves as "basically shy." Most of them don't stay that way long.

 ## What can I learn from resident advisers?

 In the residence halls on most campuses, there will be one RA for every 25 or so students. Their rooms are nearby, their doors are open, and their counsel is free.

For best results, regard your RA the same way you regard your professor, that is, as an individual to consult whenever you have a question. Don't wait until you develop a major problem to take advantage of your RA's training and expertise. RAs (again, the title may be dorm counselor or something similar) are chosen for their patience, maturity, leadership skills, and, significantly, for their knowledge of how the system works. A savvy RA can help you slice through institutional red tape and save you hours by revealing shortcuts around the academic bureaucracy. But you have to seek your RAs out; you won't get much help from them by sitting passively in your room and trying to solve your problems alone.

"I'm amazed at how few students throughout the country really utilize their resident advisers fully," one university administrator grumbled. "It's as if they pulled into a gas station, gave the attendant $10, then drove off after getting only $5 worth of gas. They're only getting half of what they've already paid for."

How much privacy will I have in the dorm?

To a great extent, it depends on whether your roommate is gone a lot, which is often the case, or is always in the room at the same time you are. If you feel a little crowded, you can juggle your own hours a bit—get up an hour before he or she does or stay up later at night. The same is true about bathroom traffic; some students find it suits them better to take their showers at unpopular hours just for the luxury of a little privacy, at 5:30 a.m., for instance, or after midnight or even in midafternoon, when almost everyone has gone to class or work.

Q Should I room with my best friend from high school?

Probably not. I've known beautiful friendships to break up that way. In the first place, just because you've confided every secret since grade 1, there's no guarantee that being together *full-time* won't grow tiresome. You can get to know each other too well. And the things you've admired most about that person can soon be eclipsed by mannerisms or habits that make you feel you're about to lose your mind if they occur just one more time! You never knew, for instance, that she gets her shiny teeth by brushing noisily ten minutes at a time, four times a day, while standing in front of the TV screen. Or that every night after he turns out the light, he methodically cracks each knuckle—all twenty of them. (Hitchcockian-type plots begin running through your head by the time he's reached number twelve in the countdown.)

Or, perhaps in fear of the unknown in your new surroundings, you stick together like Siamese twins every time you leave your room; you meet for each meal, go to parties together, even to the movies on weekends. How are you going to make new friends? Your freshman year is the best opportunity you'll have to meet the other *also* new people on your campus. Don't let that time slip past you. You and your best friend may not grow and change and accept college life at the same tempo.

Obviously many best friends from high school have become college roommates and adjusted nicely together, keeping both friendship and roommate relationship intact. In any case, it is not necessarily true that roommates *have* to be best friends. Being on good terms is possible without sharing the same interests—or the same high school history.

Q What if I simply don't like my roommate? Is it possible to change?

A Many campuses around the country have a moratorium on changing roommates during the first two weeks. After that, it may be allowed at some schools, but changes are not always possible or even desirable. Housing officials will usually try to mediate problems between roommates and resolve disputes if they can.

"If we can't," one housing administrator said, "if there is just no way the problem can be worked out—if the two people are obviously going to kill each other if they stay in the same room—then we make every effort to let them change. But much depends on the availability of space and whether another person is willing to switch. (In other words, is there a spot to move to?) Sometimes we just may not have a choice. Usually the requests drop significantly after those first two weeks when no changes are allowed. That gives them time to let the dust settle, and by the end of that period they might say, 'Well, she (or he) is not so bad after all.' "

Let me underscore that last point. Remember that one reason you've gone to college is to meet, and to try to get along with, different types of people. A law of physics—opposites attract—can apply even inside dorm rooms. So give your roommate and yourself a chance before you split up.

If all else fails, and if you do indeed feel you absolutely must change roommates in order to preserve your sanity, try finding someone else who's willing to share a room with you and still another somebody to move in with your present roommate once you leave. If you can simplify in advance the bureaucratic mechanics of the transfer, then your request is almost certain to be approved.

Q What if I am assigned a homosexual roommate?

A The incidence of homosexuality on college campuses is about the same as throughout society generally—perhaps a bit higher because campuses tend to be fairly tolerant places and because this is the age when individuals begin experimenting on many different levels. A number of students may explore gay or lesbian relationships briefly, then choose not to stay with them.

Sexual orientation is just one part of an individual's personality. If you can get past that, chances are you can find much about that person to make him or her interesting, worth knowing and liking.

You can't get AIDS from casual contact or from living in the same room. (See p. 117.) Nor are other students likely to identify you with, or embarrass you by, your roommate's affairs. Most gays, counselors tell me, tend to be discreet in their relationships.

Nevertheless, some students never are able to deal with this situation and their solution has been simply to find a new roommate. Others—and counselors and common sense suggest it can be done—work through their differences and become friends as well as roommates.

Q What is open visitation?

It's the time when members of the opposite sex are permitted to visit in dorm rooms. Many campuses have no limit on this time. Others allow some open visitation and normally permit the students in each residence hall to choose which visitation hours they prefer, as long as they don't exceed the maximum limits imposed by the institution.

Obviously a great many students like the idea of open visitation; it lets them socialize without having to spend a lot of money. Other students regard open visitation as an invasion of their privacy. There are plenty of arguments on either side, and you'll hear them all if and when your dorm is permitted to establish its own visitation policy.

Q Will I need to open my own checking account when I get to campus? Couldn't I use my hometown bank instead?

You could, but you'll find it considerably more difficult to cash a check on an out-of-town bank. Many shops and most pizza parlors just won't do it. There are places on campus where you can cash a check on your hometown bank—the bursar's office and probably a place in the student union—but these won't be open nights and weekends. As a general rule, it's better to establish an account with a bank in your college community, preferably a bank with a 24-hour-a-day automatic teller that can make your money available to you in an emergency.

If you have a choice of banks, you might do some comparison shopping before opening an account. Consider the amount of the monthly checking fee, the friendliness of the clerks, the kinds of services offered, and the locations of the bank's branch offices.

One other point: No matter where you bank, there will be times when you'll have trouble cashing a personal check. A difficult shopkeeper or department store clerk may order you to produce several items of identification and even then regard you with doubt and suspicion. Some students, especially those who have grown up in small communities or folksy neighborhoods, become utterly devastated at this kind of confrontation. It's nothing personal. The shopkeeper probably has been burned by worthless checks many times in the past and as a result considers customers guilty until proven innocent. But this is a generalized attitude and it's not directed at you personally, so don't be upset by it.

Q I've never handled my own money before. How do you balance a checkbook?

A This is a question that has baffled professors, too, for many years, so I won't promise you a quick and easy answer. I can, however, pass along advice from bankers, those no-nonsense types who regard the management of a checking account as simplicity itself. Here are their suggestions:

1. Make sure your checks are numbered consecutively. Record each check by number and amount in your checkbook register *as you write it,* not later in the day when you'll probably have forgotten the precise amount (or even the fact that you wrote the check at all).
2. *Never* write a check before your deposit has had time to get to the bank. (Checks normally take two to five business days, cash one day.) If you do, you could suffer the embarrassment of bounced checks, which also carry a nasty little penalty of something like $10 or more apiece.
3. Verify each entry as you make it. This will save you a lot of grief later on. Don't round off figures; record each item to the penny.
4. Hang on to your deposit slips, at least until you see that your deposit has been recorded on your monthly statement. Your receipt may be the only means the bank has of tracing your deposit if there is a question or a mistake.

5. Each month the bank will send your cancelled checks and a statement of your account. At this point you should reconcile your checkbook register with your statement. Examine each check and locate the entry for it in your checkbook and your bank statement, perhaps putting a tiny pencil mark beside each entry as you move along.

   Next, go back through your checkbook and add up any checks you've written that have not yet been recorded on the statement, and deduct the total from the balance listed on the statement. Add any deposits that have not yet been recorded by the bank, and deduct the service charges (the bank's fee for handling your account). Your final figures—your checkbook balance and the adjusted balance on your statement—should be exactly the same. If they aren't, redo your arithmetic and reverify each entry in your checkbook register. If your account still doesn't balance and you see no other errors, take your checkbook and your statement to the bank. You should get a prompt explanation. Do not, however, expect the bank to do your bookkeeping for you; some banks charge a fee for unraveling your tangled finances.

6. Finally, remember that your cancelled checks are your receipts and your proof of payment. Hang on to them.

Q Should I take my car to college with me? My parents don't think it's a good idea. What advice do you have?

A First, you'd better find out whether it's legal. Many colleges simply prohibit freshmen from having cars, so your problem may already be solved for you. On other campuses, freshmen may grudgingly be allowed to have cars. Parking space is usually hard to come by, however (show me a college campus and I'll show you a parking problem), and freshmen normally aren't allowed to use the better lots. The only parking spaces open to you may be, say, at the football stadium parking lot; this means you might end up having to walk or ride a shuttle bus to and from a distant part of the campus each time you want to use your car. Or—and this can be a real pain—you can scramble for one of the few spaces available on the city streets, where you are subject to local police regulations. Your car, in other words, may be more trouble than it's worth.

If you do take your car to campus, you most probably will be required to register it with campus security or the local police. Failure to do so can result in severe disciplinary action.

Another tip: Never let an upperclass student register your car in order to get a higher priority parking sticker. Such subterfuges are usually found out, and the culprits are dealt with harshly.

Q Should I take my bicycle along or plan on using public transportation?

A Bicycles are convenient, quick, and relatively cheap, and they provide an almost perfect means of transportation on many campuses. At some schools, however, students complain of problems with traffic, storage, and theft and say they wish they had left their bikes at home. If you can find out about the bike situation on campus before you go, that's great. Otherwise, the bicycle decision is one you probably should postpone until after you've been on campus for a while and have been able to assess your needs. If you do bring your bike, bring along a sturdy lock as well. And check with campus police, who will probably want you to register your bicycle with them.

Larger schools usually have buses to shuttle students from one part of the campus to another. These shuttles are sometimes slow and often crowded, but they are generally reliable and the service is free or provided at minimal cost.

Unless your campus is a tiny one in a rural area, there's a good chance that you can make do with public transportation—city buses or trains that connect you with the rest of the world.

Hitchhiking, a favorite mode of travel for students in a gentler time, is now illegal in many jurisdictions and dangerous in all of them. Don't try it.

Q I've always had trouble with my weight. How can I escape gaining the dreaded Freshman 10?

A The Freshman 10, sometimes known as the Freshman Lard, refers to the hefty weight gain associated with going away to college. Women especially seem to fear it. The affliction is not fatal but it can be avoided. Here's a summary of advice from some determinedly slim students I know:

- First of all, don't reward yourself with junk food! You've studied 4 solid hours for an economics test, it's nearly midnight, and someone is sending out for pizzas. "You've worked hard," says your roommate. "You *deserve* nourishment." But listen instead to what your scales are telling you, and they're telling you "No! No!"
- Rent a small refrigerator (nearly every campus provides this service) and stock it with low-calorie sodas and fruit juices. Keep a hot pot in your room and fix soup or bouillon for lunch and late-night snacks. Instead of reaching for that doughnut or Danish in the breakfast line, try a grapefruit or a hard-boiled egg, toast, and coffee or tea (without sugar). Drink a large glass of water before dinner. If the main course is something fried, skip it and go with a fruit plate or vegetable plate instead. Don't try to starve yourself. Just eat good healthy food.
- Exercise is important, too, even if it's only trotting up and down the corridors or stairs of your dorm for 20 minutes a night.
- Seek out friends who are also watching their calorie intake; mutual support and reinforcement can make a big difference.

It *is* possible to defeat the Dreaded 10. Think how nice it will be when you go home and your friends say, "Gee, you look great! I thought you'd have gained a ton by now!"

Q What problems might I face in living off campus?

A For all its homely image, the college dormitory room remains a most efficient place for student living. Classroom buildings and the library are usually within easy walking distance. Though rarely elegant, residence hall cafeterias are convenient, and they serve up decent meals that are nourishing and relatively inexpensive. And for the most part, dorm atmosphere is lively and agreeable.

Yet many students are bored to tears with it. Each year tens of thousands of them trek off campus in search of the apartment of their dreams. For some, the dream develops into marvelous reality as they discover in apartment living the freedom and independence they had been wishing for. Others, however, see their dream turn into a nightmare.

Should you take the plunge? Before answering that question, housing directors warn, ask yourself another one: Can you afford it? Residence hall costs are constant and predictable. Apartment expenses won't be. Can your budget stand it if your utility bills go up another $35 a month? What if grocery prices keep rising?

Consider the matter of transportation. How will you get back and forth to classes and the supermarket? If your answer is "by car," can you afford the upkeep? If your answer is "by bicycle," what provisions are you making for rotten weather? These problems are certainly not insurmountable, but they do require some thought.

Location—closely related to affordability—is another factor. Apartments and rooms within easy walking distance of the campus have become expensive. The housing is cheaper miles away from campus, but the downside comes in longer commuting time and a certain remoteness from friends and campus activities.

"And then," warns one college housing director, "there is the question of the facilities, particularly the older places close to the campuses. Landlords don't always keep the rooms and apartments in good repair, and some students, especially those from nice homes, have trouble adjusting."

What he's saying is that your apartment may turn out to be a dump. Largely because of that, students often find themselves embroiled in disputes over damage deposits. This is the money the renter must put up ahead of time to cover any damage to the apartment during the rental period. Some deposits amount to the equivalent of a full month's rent or more; others may be a flat $100 or $200. Frequently, a landlord will insist on keeping the deposit, alleging that the student damaged the apartment, while the student will claim that the damage had been done beforehand. Since the landlord is a pro and the student is an amateur, the student usually comes out second best. (One suggestion: Write up a list of the damage you find when you move in. Date it, send it to the landlord, and keep a copy for your records. It's not a guarantee there won't be problems, but it should help.)

Some students trip themselves up by not reading or fully understanding their lease agreement. A lease may run for an entire year, for example, while the student who signed it planned to live in the apartment only for the nine-month academic term; unless the place can be sublet for the summer (no easy task in some communities), the student could get stuck. Or perhaps he or she innocently brings a puppy to the apartment, only to learn that the lease specifically forbids pets.

Despite the negative aspects—and clearly there are some—many students cherish the privacy, the freedom, and the further advance into adulthood they see embodied in their student apartments. For them, apartment life opens up an entire new world, one where they set up housekeeping, cook the kinds of meals they want when they want them, arrange furniture, stock a pantry, and manage a home of their own. It's a maturing experience, and thousands of students find it to be a joyous one as well.

Q I'm going to school in my hometown. Should I live at home or on campus?

A This decision, a big one, is between you and your folks, and it will hinge on specific circumstances I don't know anything about. As a broad generalization, however, let me offer the following: Freshmen who live at home tend to make better grades and spend less money. Freshmen who live on campus tend to have more fun and grow up faster.

Living at home allows you to retain comfortable, familiar surroundings while easing yourself gradually into college life. Because you aren't trying to adjust to everything at once, you can concentrate more on your studies. There won't be the distractions (a noisy dorm floor, a roommate whose lifestyle may be wildly different from your own, the logistical problems of doing your laundry and getting your clothes mended) that drain your energies away from academics.

Even with commuting costs, you'll find living at home almost certainly cheaper than living on campus, and this is a deciding factor in many cases. The fun you might have had living in the dorm could be clouded by guilt if you feel you're placing too great a financial strain on the rest of the family.

An alternative solution might be for you to rent a room in someone's house near the campus. This can be the thriftiest housing move available. A furnished room averages between $150 and $200 a month, usually, and that cost probably will include all utilities. It may also—but won't always—include house and kitchen privileges as well. You may be able to reduce the rent dramatically by mowing the lawn or doing household chores, babysitting whatever. As with any housing arrangement, there are tradeoffs; by renting a room in a house you may miss out on some socializing in the dorm. On the other hand, the privacy will be a blessing to the serious scholar.

By the same token, moving onto the campus has its distinct advantages also. You'll learn as much simply by living with all those assorted characters in your dorm as you will in any academic subject. Personal development, the kind that comes from coping with new surroundings and from managing on your own, is part of your education too. Strange as it may seem, the individuals in your dorm or fraternity or sorority house will occupy positions of prominence in the years ahead. Deep friendships and good memories develop at this time in your life.

So if you can't move onto the campus even for one semester, just for the experience of "going off to college," you ought to find ways to involve yourself in campus life. Try a service or academic club in order to establish a base of operations on the campus. Another good bet is joining the association of commuting students at your college. This group will, at a minimum, field intramural sports teams, throw a round of parties, and run a slate of candidates in student election campaigns. Without question, it is more difficult to become immersed in college life while living at home, but tens of thousands of students every year prove it can be done.

Q In general, what changes can I expect as I adjust to college?

A College freshmen share many of the concerns of young people everywhere: money (or lack of it), love, roommates, growing up, and leaving home. There is a lot of change going on; significantly, however, the really important changes in freshmen seem to occur outside the classroom rather than inside it.

The academic work is important, certainly. It's the reason for going to college in the first place. But the freshmen I encounter are far better prepared for dealing with their studies than they are for living on their own. Many freshmen don't handle their newfound independence very well; in some colleges the dropout rate for freshmen is 25 percent or higher. Those who do survive the freshman year are apt to sum it up with a statement like, "Gee, I've really changed. I'm hardly the same person I was in high school."

A study of freshmen at the University of Iowa, conducted by a research team headed by psychologist Patricia M. King and reported in the *University of Iowa Spectator,* found that only 1 freshman in 5 felt that the important experiences of the freshman year had to do with intellectual development. The other 80 percent cited as their most important experiences (1) their involvement with other people, (2) the development of their own sense of identity, and (3) the formation of moral principles and practical skills to guide their lives. Here is what some of them had to say:

- "One of the most important experiences I . . . had was meeting a person who became my friend. It was important for me because I had never met someone who had such a different background from mine."
- "My first accident (I broke my toe) . . . showed me that my parents weren't around. And also that when bad things happen you can depend on your roommates and neighbors."
- "This one is very personal, but very important to me—my first time truly falling in love. It gave me hope for the future, kept me going through rough times, taught me a lot about myself and my boyfriend, and made me give a little more love back to my parents and friends."

21

- For one of the respondents, choosing to go to Mass on his own for the first time was the most significant experience of the freshman year: "It proved to me that I did have faith, and it wasn't that my parents made me go to church. I felt a sense of pride—or more . . . I thought that my faith, which I had early doubted, was very real."
- Another student was most strongly affected by the realization that she wasn't the smartest person in the school: "I've always been good in school and I got good grades, so I came here expecting to get very few B's. That's the only part I got right. I'm getting the rest of my grades as C's instead of the A's I had expected. For a while I thought I would adjust and get perfect tests, but thought again and realized that I'm not a genius. That helped."

Dr. King summarized her findings this way: "It seems to me that you (freshmen) have to establish yourself in a community, you have to have friends, you have to be comfortable both with yourself and with others, before you can really thrive intellectually."

This study at Iowa supports an old theory of many educators, namely, that students, and especially freshmen, learn a good deal more from each other than they ever do from us on the faculty. Here's what Canadian scholar Stephan Butler Leacock had to say on just this subject many years ago, back in the days of mellow cigars and lively conversation: "If I were founding a university I would first found a smoking room; then when I had a little more money in hand I would found a dormitory; then after that, or more probably with it, a decent reading room and a library. After that, if I still had more money that I couldn't use, I would hire a professor and get some textbooks."

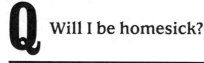

Will I be homesick?

Probably. If you're living away from home for the first time, and if your home situation is any good at all, it would be unusual if you weren't mildly or even terribly homesick at times. This is natural. Don't worry about it.

A subtler and possibly more painful malady you may encounter is the longing to turn back the clock. This can't be done, and some of the saddest souls on any campus are those college freshmen whose thoughts, wishes, and endless conversations dwell on their glorious moments in high school.

How long your homesickness/nostalgia lasts depends on how determined you are to thrust yourself fully into your new surroundings. The best way to do that? Pretend that you're going to be on your campus for the rest of your life. Forget that you'll be leaving college in a few years. For now, this is where you live. Put down roots. Adopt the campus and the community as your own. Learn their geography, their history, their sociology. You've made the physical move to college; now make the intellectual and emotional move as well.

This doesn't mean you won't miss your old friends, or that you should sever ties with them. On the contrary: Some of your happiest moments will come on visits home when you see your friends again, compare notes with them, and talk for hours about the lives you're beginning to make for yourselves. Your friends are growing and changing too, and it will be fascinating for you to watch how they turn out. In the meantime, you've got a new world to adjust to. Don't let it pass you by.

Q How do I deal with my parents now?

A Maintaining contact is really not that difficult if you just do it, if only by writing a short note or making a phone call once a week (collect, of course). You aren't required to write an epistle; a postcard or a fold-a-note will do, even one sentence just to let them know you are in reasonably good health, that you're thinking of them. Parents rarely subscribe to the notion that no news is good news. Yet for the most part they are notoriously easy to please, just as long as they hear *something*. The problem is that you have so much to tell them about—new ideas, new friends, a flurry of activities—that you think it's impossible to clear away enough time to write a long thoughtful letter when you have a major paper due on Friday, a psych exam tomorrow, an oral report in English for Monday, and a date Saturday night.

What's the answer? A small piece of paper, even a postcard saying "I'm snowed under, folks, but otherwise doing fine. Love, Me." Mail one of these every Monday. Parents can be stalled almost indefinitely as long as *something* comes in the mail from you periodically. You could also reach out by phone, preferably on Saturday or Sunday when the rates are cheaper. Write a note to yourself on your calendar: "Monday: Letter home," or "Saturday: Phone home." Then *do* it. You won't believe how happy you can make someone.

Consider inviting your parents for a weekend. They may not be able to come, but think how pleased they'll be to have been asked. What if they *do* come? Then see to it that they have a good time, that they feel you are proud to show them off. Be prepared to listen to their advice, but don't feel that your private territory or your new way of life is being invaded. Realize that you're going through a natural, if frequently painful, development—wanting to be with your parents, yet wanting to become independent of them at the same time. Your frustration and uncertainty may be compounded by guilt, especially if you know your parents may be making a great personal sacrifice to help pay for your college expenses. The first few weeks are usually the worst; your ideas, your emotions, your entire personality could swing pretty far in a new direction. But *don't* tell your parents, on their first visit, that you have decided to change your religion or adopt a new life-style because of something your prof said in Philosophy 101. There's plenty of time for that. Give your folks a chance to realize you will inevitably be moving in other directions as time goes on. To your utter astonishment, they'll probably understand. After all, they went through some kind of weaning process themselves a generation ago.

One other suggestion: Ask your folks for a subscription to your hometown newspaper or, at least, to the Sunday edition. This will keep you posted on issues and people you know about and provide you with plenty of things to talk about when you do communicate with your parents. It will also assure you of getting something in your mailbox, which is no small matter. College students get lonely too.

CHAPTER 2

HITTING THE BOOKS

You have had twelve years of experience as a student already, and college classes, with teachers to figure out and subject matter to be learned, aren't that much different from what you've grown accustomed to in high school. In other words, as you'll be pleasantly surprised to discover, the academic adjustment, despite its obvious importance, is probably the easiest one you'll be called upon to make during your freshman year. Still, there are some things you'll want to know, such as:

Q How will I know which classes to select?

A The obvious answer is to take courses that interest you, that are in a field you might like to major in, or that are prerequisites to courses you will want to take later. Take courses in areas you never studied in high school; colleges offer many more subjects than the typical high school curriculum has. Also ask upperclass students; most will be more than happy to give their opinions of the interesting courses and the interesting professors. A dynamic lecturer can turn a topic you never thought you'd like into a fascinating semester.

In addition, you will be assigned to a faculty adviser whose job it is to assist you in choosing your courses and planning your overall program. Be warned, however. The faculty adviser is just that, an adviser, not someone who dictates your class schedule to you. The actual selection of courses will be yours and yours alone. There are lots of classes available, and you'll have plenty of freedom to pick and choose. That's the good news. The bad news is that if anything goes wrong, such as your failing to fulfill college requirements by the end of four years, it's *your* fault, even if your adviser's signature appeared on all your schedule cards.

For example, suppose your college has a rule that all students must complete four courses in a foreign language. Each semester, for reasons that seem good at the time but probably aren't, you decide to postpone enrolling in language classes. Then, in the final weeks of your senior year, a records clerk discovers that you haven't completed the foreign language requirement and therefore you cannot graduate. You scream in protest, "But my faculty adviser never made me take a foreign language!" Objection overruled. No matter what the adviser said or didn't say, the ultimate responsibility—that is to say the blame—is yours. No degree.

So make certain you read carefully and understand fully the requirements as spelled out in the catalog. Be sure you know how *your* college defines credit hours and whether your college sets requirements in terms of hours, credits, courses, or otherwise. The catalog in effect when you enroll as a freshman is your compact with the institution. Fulfill the requirements and you'll get your diploma.

Q What can I expect from my faculty adviser?

A At a minimum, you should be able to count on your adviser to provide accurate, up-to-date information about college regulations and to explain various alternatives in course selection as well as make plain to you the possible consequences of your decisions. Most faculty advisers do more than this. They take a personal interest in your career and educational goals, and they monitor your progress from one term to the next. The better advisers are also prompt about referring you to service agencies (the counseling center, the placement office, a learning skills lab, tutors, etc.) if and when you need help. The faculty adviser can write recommendations for you when you're applying for a job or a place in graduate or professional school. And, not infrequently, students and faculty advisers become friends as well.

Q What if I don't agree with my faculty adviser?

A It is possible that you simply won't like your faculty adviser. Or you may distrust the advice you're getting. This happens, and let's face it, some faculty advisers are not as well informed on course changes, new requirements, alternatives, and so on as they might be. For whatever reason, if you don't feel comfortable with your adviser you can request and usually get another one. I say "usually" here because the department chair or associate dean or whoever is in charge of assigning advisers wants to divide the load evenly among the faculty and therefore may not think it wise to do any shifting at that moment. If your request for a change of adviser does get turned down, and if you feel strongly about it, head directly for the dean of the college.

The advising procedure is not as contentious as this passage may suggest. Advising should take place in a friendly and helpful atmosphere and for the most part, it does.

Q What happens at registration?

A Each semester or each quarter, college administrators attempt to let thousands of students fit themselves into hundreds of courses, to honor the ardent desires of students for a wide selection of subjects, all offered at convenient hours and places, while at the same time respecting harsh limits imposed by operating budgets, the size of the faculty, and available classroom and lab space. It is an incredibly complicated business, and the wonder is that registration works at all. Somehow, in the larger sense, it does work. At the individual student level, however, there can be disappointments. You will need patience, careful planning, a sense of humor, and a certain amount of luck in order to survive registration with your schedule intact.

While the exact procedure at your campus will be fully explained to you during freshman orientation, this is more or less what you can expect. At the outset, you'll attend an advising session to be briefed on college requirements and to receive some help in planning your course schedule. During this meeting you'll be given a copy of the schedule of courses, listing class information, and you'll then be directed to fill out your first choice of class sections. It's a good bet that some of your choices will be filled already, so you should select some alternative courses as backups. Somebody official (probably your faculty adviser) will then check over your proposed schedule and sign it.

Next, you'll pick up your registration packet, which is usually a large envelope that contains the forms you'll need in order to complete the process. With these forms in hand, you're now ready to head for registration itself, which will probably be in the gymnasium or student union ballroom. In this large crowded area, you'll discover that each academic department (English, chemistry, etc.) will have its own clearly identified table. Present your packet at the department tables offering the classes you want to take. (This is not as easy as it sounds; there will probably be waiting lines at many tables.) A department clerk will check to see whether the class you want has vacancies. If you are able to enroll for the class, the clerk will add your name to the roster and initial your packet. If, however, the class is closed, you'll need to hold everything until you've selected another one. This often requires rearranging your entire schedule, a process that can take a while. Again, you should have alternatives in mind for just such a crisis. (Many schools also have waiting lists for courses with limited enrollment, and, in some cases, it's possible to gain entry to a course by talking directly to the professor.)

You'll eventually be admitted to enough classes to fill your schedule. Now it's time to check out. Somebody will clear you at the exit (the route may remind you of a cattle chute), making certain your schedule is in order (that you haven't signed up for two classes that meet at the same time, for example).

It's possible that your tuition, lab fees, and other charges will be assessed at this point, so you might have to stop at the cashier's desk and pay up. Your financial aid check, if you have one coming, might be collected here also.

Finally, someone may need to take an official photo of you and issue your student ID card. You might also be asked to fill out additional forms, such as a student directory/phone book card, but this won't take long. There will be other tables after this, mostly for various clubs and service groups that want to recruit you for membership, but these stops are optional. For all practical purposes, you're done.

This describes a "cafeteria" registration pattern that is followed by many larger schools. It may not happen quite this way at your college, but you get the idea.

Many colleges and universities have moved to a system of preregistration, which lets you submit your course preferences (sometimes with alternatives) or enter your schedule into the campus computer and thus avoid the hassle of securing individual departmental approvals at the gym. Completed weeks before the new semester starts (often in the summer for entering freshmen), the preregistration system gives the administration more time to adjust teaching loads and classroom assignments. It allows the college to add more sections for courses that are in great demand or to consolidate or even cancel low-demand classes. If a course you want to take is canceled or you are closed out of part of your schedule for some reason, you are notified before the semester begins so that you can prepare to pick up additional classes during the add/drop/change period.

As a general rule, it's best to register early. Although some colleges process first the course requests of students with the most credits (i.e., seniors), still others do it on a first-come, first-served basis. At the latter, if your campus has preregistration, hustle in for your advising appointment as soon as possible; the quicker your schedule is approved, the sooner you'll be able to nail down your place in the top choice of classes. If your school runs the "cafeteria" type of registration in the gymnasium, you might be able to wangle a job as a student clerk, since clerks are normally permitted to register first.

In any event, be resourceful enough to choose alternative classes just in case your first choices are closed. If you assume that your original schedule will be shot down and you make contingency plans accordingly, then any damage that might be done during registration can be kept to a minimum.

Q What study aids will I need to buy?

A The shelves of your campus bookstore will be lined with attractive, tempting materials, many of which are no doubt useful, but at least in a general sense, you can get by with purchasing only a dictionary, a thesaurus, and a scholarly style manual.

If you can possibly afford one, buy a typewriter. It doesn't have to be a word processor or even an expensive electric model. A used, reconditioned manual typewriter (there are many of these on the market, very moderately priced) can do wonders for your writing assignments and, consequently, for your grades. It's also helpful for batting out those quick, and probably overdue, letters home.

You will need additional study aids in particular courses, a French-English dictionary, for example, if you're enrolled in a French class; some ledger paper and balance sheets for Accounting I; and so on, but hold off buying these until your professor tells you specifically which materials he or she prefers.

Q What should I bring to class with me?

A A notebook, certainly (either a large, all-in-one loose-leaf notebook with section dividers or a number of smaller separate notebooks, one for each course), and a supply of pencils and ballpoint pens. You may need to lug along your textbook, especially if the professor refers to it during the lecture, and it's not a bad idea to have a small, paperback dictionary with you for days when you'll be doing in-class writing. If all this proves to be unwieldy, you may decide to buy a backpack or bookbag—inexpensive, useful, and very popular.

Q What questions should I ask on the first day of class?

A If you've survived registration and learned where the buildings are, you probably think you're prepared for classes to begin. Not quite. There's one more thought you need to bear in mind and it's an unsettling one: Many professors don't explain things very well.

Most of us have a great deal of training in a particular subject area, such as recent U.S. history, galactic astronomy, or biochemistry, but very little, if any, training in the techniques of teaching. Your high school teachers were probably better organized and better skilled in the nuts and bolts of imparting information than your college professors will be. This means you must learn to take an active role in your courses right from the start. You won't be spoon-fed.

On the first day of class your professor will probably distribute and discuss the outline for the course. He or she may explain all that you need to know. But if not, ask the questions that will take care of loose ends. Don't count on other students to ask for you; students can be notoriously passive, especially early in the semester. Before you leave the first class meeting, you should fully understand the following:

Objectives. What are the professor's goals for the course? What approach will be followed? Perhaps your Spanish course will deal with literature, and you thought the emphasis was going to be on conversational skills; there may be time for you to switch your class schedule accordingly.

Grading. How will your progress be evaluated? How many exams are planned? Will the final exam be comprehensive, that is, will it cover the entire course content or just the material presented since the last test? How much weight will be attached to the final exam? What kinds of tests will there be: essay, true or false, multiple choice? Does the professor use a strict grading scale (93 to 100 is an A, for example) or will the grades be "curved"?

Outside work. How many assignments such as papers, book reviews, case studies, etc., will be given? How much time are they likely to require? You will have to take into account the work expected of you in other courses to decide whether you will be able to handle the load. How much of your grade depends on your performance in these outside assignments?

Attendance. Some professors carefully monitor classroom attendance, though most simply ignore it. There may well be no general, campuswide rule (not one often enforced, anyway), so you'll need to become familiar with each professor's policy. Some profs will reduce your grade for excessive absences (find out precisely what "excessive" means). Others will give unannounced tests ("pop quizzes"), and students who are absent get a zero for that day. Be realistic enough to assume you'll miss class from time to time, because of the flu, if nothing else. Make certain you know (1) whether those absences are going to hurt you, and if so how much, and (2) if makeups are possible.

Office hours. Find out the times when the professor will be available in his or her campus study. Professors are not always around when you need them; they may be holed up in the library doing research or at home grading papers. If your professor doesn't tell you on the first day, ask him or her how you can arrange a meeting should a problem develop with the course.

Costs. Some subjects are expensive. You may have to buy a dozen or more paperbacks for a lit class, for example, or shell out hefty lab fees in some science courses. An introductory course in photography might involve an extra $300 in camera rental, darkroom fees, chemicals, film, and paper. Find out just what the additional costs will be; you may be able to reschedule an expensive class for another semester when your budget is in better shape.

In sum, remember that you are the consumer and that you have every right to know what you're getting yourself into when you sign up for a class. Don't be bashful about asking questions. Many professors have a bit of trouble getting back into the teaching groove that first day—I know I do—and they may well overlook some important point that should be explained to the class. It's up to you to help out.

 What if I just don't like a course? Or a professor? How can I change my schedule?

Your class schedule is not necessarily an ironclad contract, at least not at the beginning of the semester. You can make adjustments fairly easily during the drop/add/change period—called Shopping Period at Yale, for example—which lasts anywhere from a few days to a few weeks, depending on the college. During this time the paperwork involved in making changes is generally minimal. Later on it gets more difficult to add a course; you'll need the professor's permission, which probably won't be given after a week or so of class meetings, plus the approval of your adviser and/or the dean. You can take much more time—a month or longer, usually—to drop a course without having the fact that you withdrew recorded on your transcript.

Many students intentionally sign up for more courses than they intend to take, go to the first meetings of each class, size up the profs and the requirements, and then drop a class or two to trim their schedule down to manageable proportions. Remember that your professor is ethically obliged to explain at the first class meeting how much work is expected of you, how you'll be evaluated, and so on. If this information terrifies you (or bores you or infuriates you), consider unloading that particular course and picking up another one.

Another nice thing about drop/add/change is that often a class that had been closed will open up a bit as students drop out after the first few days. You might be able to slip into a course at this time that you couldn't get into before. Go to the first few class meetings, and tell the professor you're interested in taking the course if space opens up. Even if enough people don't drop it, many professors don't mind an extra interested student.

Q Is there a dress code? What do students wear to class?

A These days, student dress codes are rare. However, a number of colleges, mostly church-related, still have them, and if you're enrolling in one of these institutions the requirements will be fully explained to you before classes begin. Everywhere else, you're pretty much free to wear whatever suits your fancy, provided you don't break any state laws of common decency or violate some local health ordinances, such as going barefoot in the dining area.

Campus styles these days range from punk to preppy, with many gradations in between. You occasionally see a student wearing a coat and tie, but this ensemble is almost always connected to a job or scholarship interview. You will probably want to have some dressier outfits for special occasions. For classes, however, the casual clothes you wore in high school should do nicely.

Q What if I'm late for class?

A Tiptoe in anyway. It's possible you may be momentarily embarrassed by the slight interruption you cause—especially if the professor halts the lecture to inquire "Enjoyed your breakfast this morning, did you?"—but that's a small price to pay for catching at least a portion of what could be an important class meeting. You may not get all the material that has been covered that day, but at a minimum you will pick up the emphasis, which is a useful thing to know when you're preparing for the next exam.

Consistent tardiness, however, is a form of rudeness and should be avoided. If you have real problems getting there on time—your previous class meets at the other end of the campus, say, and the teacher in that one tends to run overtime—then explain the problem to both professors concerned. In many cases, nothing can be done about it (though there is the outside chance that the long-winded prof in your earlier class might become more conscious of the clock that governs the rest of us), but your teachers will appreciate your intentions, if not your timing.

Q What happens if I miss a class?

A Probably nothing. That is, nothing tangible and nothing of immediate consequence. While your college or university may have something called an attendance regulation, it is probably written in lofty, general, unenforceable language. At Colgate University, for example, the policy reads this way: "Students who have enrolled at Colgate have made a commitment to participate in the educational program of the institution. Attendance at classes is an important part of that commitment. . . ." And at Cornell: "Students are expected to be present throughout each term at all meetings of courses for which they are registered."

In practical terms, though, each professor sets his or her own ground rules for attendance. Some professors check the roll at each class meeting. Most don't. This means, in effect, that if you want to sleep through your 8 a.m. English class or catch a matinee during your biology lab, you can. There won't be parents to mobilize you or snippy school administrators to question your whereabouts during class time; it's highly unlikely that the prof will mark you absent or for that matter even notice whether you're there or not. If you do attend class, in other words, it will be because (warning: pious words ahead) you are assuming the responsibility, as an adult and a young professional, of making the most of your educational opportunities.

There are other, perhaps more pertinent, reasons you shouldn't skip classes. For one thing, you may lose out on something important. An advisee of mine came to me almost in tears after she got back an hour exam paper with a 60 on it—a grade low enough to kill her chances of getting an A for the course. "It was that one class I cut," she said, grimly. "He asked ten questions on the test, and four of them—the four I missed—he covered in that one lecture. I borrowed some notes, but they weren't any good. *If I had been there,* I'd have understood."

In smaller classes, a high degree of student involvement is expected. If you aren't present, you can't pull your weight. Your professor may not go through the ritual of checking the roll each time, but he or she jolly well knows who's contributing to the class discussion and who isn't, and your attendance record, directly or indirectly, will be reflected in your course grade.

If you are absent, make an effort to find out what was covered from someone else in the class, preferably from someone who takes good notes. Don't, as a general rule, ask the professor to fill you in. The prof can't very well conduct one class for everybody else and a separate one for you, and most of us react coldly to a student who says, "Sorry I wasn't in class yesterday. Did I miss anything?" Early in the semester, get the names and phone numbers of classmates who look as though they can be counted on to brief you reliably on material presented in your absence.

If you miss several class meetings, say you had the flu or you took a long road trip with the golf team, and you sense your absences might be noticed, then it's a good idea to explain briefly to the professor. This is good public relations on your part, and the prof, in turn, may volunteer a useful tip for you, such as, "We hit chapter three pretty hard on Friday. Be sure you understand those charts on page 79; you may be asked about them on the next quiz."

Q What if I already know the material in a course?

A You might be able to challenge by special examination and get credit for the course without having to sit through it. Courses on many campuses are available for challenge credit regardless of whether you have studied the material independently, are currently enrolled, or have acquired the skills through experience. These special examinations, which are comparable to the final exams in the actual classes, are developed and administered by the academic departments concerned. There is usually no charge for these exams, so you have nothing to lose by trying.

As an example, consider the case of Janet, who is a history major but also a camera enthusiast. She's shot pictures under all types of conditions, processed the film herself, even had some of her photos published. The fine arts department of her college offers a course in photography, covering subject material and techniques she's already mastered. Because she needs to pick up some more credits to avoid having to go to summer school, Janet decides to ask the fine arts department for a special examination in this course. She supports her request with a portfolio of her best photographs. If the chairperson believes Janet is reasonably prepared, he or she will arrange an examination for her. In this case, the test would probably include a photo assignment as well as a written quiz covering terms and procedures. If she passes, credit for the photography course will be entered on her transcript.

Credit by examination can thus help qualified students get their degree more quickly, escape superfluous basic requirements, or simply buy more time.

It is also possible to use knowledge acquired elsewhere to bypass prerequisites and move immediately into an advanced subject. (A prerequisite is a requirement that must be met before a course is taken.) Suppose you spent last year as a part-time intern in your city's Department of Human Resources, where you became keenly interested in social work. You want to study the subject further, but you find out that all the upper-level courses in your school's social work department carry a prerequisite called Introduction to Social Services. If you can convince the professor that you're already familiar with the content of the introductory course, he or she probably will let you skip that one altogether and enroll in the advanced class.

Q What are placement exams?

A In certain subjects, especially math and languages, students can qualify for advanced placement and/or credit by scoring above a certain minimum on departmental exams given during freshman orientation. The idea here is simply to allow you to enroll at the level of study that is appropriate for you.

You may decide not to accept advanced standing (your placement test score indicates you qualify for a second-year course in German, while you would prefer to review some of the material taught in first-year classes), but the option is a useful one for those who wish to take advantage of it.

Q How are Advanced Placement exams handled?

A Most colleges and universities participate in the College Board Advanced Placement Program and will award credit for those toughie AP courses you took in high school. A score of 3 or better on the American History AP exam, for example, may earn you six semester hours of credit at your college, spring you loose from the history portion of your general studies requirements, and provide you with immediate entry into the more challenging upper-level offerings in the history department. The policies vary somewhat from one campus to another and even among departments on any one campus (some schools or departments may require an essay in addition, for example), but many bright high school students each year receive credit, exemptions from requirements, or both via the AP route. One other note: Your test results won't automatically follow you, so make certain to have them forwarded to your college registrar's office.

Q What is CLEP credit and how can I get it?

A The College-Level Examination Program (CLEP) is a nationally recognized means of acquiring college or university credit for what you may have learned through on-the-job experience, extensive reading, correspondence study, television courses, and the like.

The CLEP examinations, usually 90-minute multiple-choice tests, are offered in both General and Subject areas. The General examinations are available in English, history, the humanities, mathematics, natural sciences, and social sciences. Subject exams are offered in a variety of specific areas. In business, for example, there are tests in computers and data processing, introduction to management, introductory accounting, introductory business law, and introductory marketing. Other subject areas include composition and literature, foreign languages, science, and mathematics. These tests are designed to measure both knowledge and achievement; if you can prove through one or more of these tests that your knowledge compares with that of the typical college student who has had the specific course work, you can receive the credit without having to take the class.

Each college determines just which CLEP tests it will accept, the minimum passing score allowed, and the amount of credit it will award. Some institutions, for example, will accept CLEP Subject exams but not General exams. There is a fee for administering and processing CLEP tests, which are given at regular intervals throughout the country. To find out what the CLEP policy is at a particular college, check with the admissions office or the counseling and testing center. For more information about the program in general, write to CLEP, Box 1822, Princeton, New Jersey 08541.

CLEP is worth investigating, especially for older students whose life and career experiences may be converted into college credit. No matter where or how you have learned, you can take CLEP tests and, if the results are acceptable to your college, be rewarded for your efforts.

Q I've always had trouble getting papers done on time. What if I miss an assignment due date?

A The tennis coach I had in high school insisted that his players always hit forehand drives precisely when the ball had bounced waist high. "But coach," one of us asked him, "what if the ball comes at us so we *can't* hit it waist high?" The coach was unimpressed. "Then all you have to do," he said, "is move your carcass to the spot where you *can*." So there. What if you miss an assignment due date? Don't miss it, that's all.

Class assignments normally are given well in advance. You have no immediate pressure to begin work on them, and the temptation to procrastinate is overwhelming. Then—wham! Not only is that English essay due tomorrow, but there's a major test in biology Wednesday afternoon, an in-class presentation in French on Thursday, and you suddenly find you've fallen dangerously behind in econ. Grade averages are made—and lost—amid just such crises.

One cold winter morn I was visiting a friend on the set of NBC's Today show. Knowing he'd been at work since 3:30 a.m., I asked how he was able to discipline himself to wake up and function at that unearthly hour. "The discipline isn't in getting up early," he said. "The discipline comes in forcing yourself to go to bed early the night before." That same reasoning applies to meeting assignment due dates. The virtue is not in the Herculean effort you put forth that desperate night before the deadline; it's in the steady, patient work you do on the project in the days and weeks well before the paper is due.

If you turn a paper in late, expect at the very least to have your grade lowered as a penalty. Some professors refuse to accept late papers at all; they will return them to you ungraded or toss them in the wastebasket and record a zero for you instead. Unless there is a legitimate emergency, one that can be verified, don't ask the professor for special treatment. He or she doesn't want to be put in the position of having one set of rules for everybody else and a separate one for you. Bear in mind that the deadlines you face in college are nothing compared to those you'll face later in life.

Q How can I learn to take good lecture notes?

A The lecture is still the most common form of instruction in most courses, and the typical college student will sit through literally hundreds of hours of lectures during an undergraduate career. Most students actually stay awake throughout these lectures, and a good number listen hard and try to learn. Yet only a relative few ever develop an adequate system for taking lecture notes, and those who don't wonder why they don't do better on examinations.

Good note-taking is positively essential to good academic progress. There is, of course, no one perfect system for taking lecture notes. Each individual eventually develops a personal code of abbreviations, patterns, outline forms, and so on. Nevertheless, there are some general guidelines that can help make those long lecture hours more productive:

Do your assigned reading beforehand. Even if you don't have time to study the material thoroughly, at least try to read it over the night before class. If tomorrow's lecture in Principles of Economics will deal with supply-side theory, for example, use the reading assignment to become familiar with the terms and concepts your lecturer will be using. There's nothing more bewildering to a student or more frustrating to a teacher than when the lecturer and the class are tuned to different wavelengths.

Get to class on time. Often the professor will state the objectives and outline the lecture at the very beginning of the hour. The professor may also start out by offering to answer questions and clear up loose ends from last time. This is your opportunity to clarify points you were unsure about previously.

Look for significance. Throughout the lecture, keep asking yourself: Why is this being emphasized? Of all the possible statements that could be made on a given topic, why these? A lecture is not just an explanation of a subject; it is the professor's interpretation of the importance of that subject. You may or may not always agree with the professor's interpretation, but you need to know what it is, for exam purposes if nothing else, and you need to get it into your notes.

Listen for organizational cues. Some professors write out their lectures word for word; others don't write anything. Most, however, will speak from outline notes. With a little practice, you can quickly pick up how the professor has organized the lecture material. Listen for such phrases as "the second reason for the change is," or "a third important factor is," or "still another consideration is." These lead-in lines reveal something about the professor's own thought patterns and attitudes.

Don't try to write too much. If you do, you'll probably get bogged down in details and miss something really important. Avoid trying to recapture the professor's sentences word for word; he or she can talk faster than you can write. Jot down specific figures that seem important and summarize the main points as tersely as you can as the lecturer presents them.

Be sure you understand terminology. Each subject has its own jargon. In economics, for example, some essential terms include GNP, cartel, marginal productivity, and equilibrium; it's almost a whole new language. Make sure these terms are properly defined in your notes. If the professor uses an unfamiliar term during the lecture, ask a question for clarification. If you don't ask, he or she will probably assume you don't have a problem, and moments later you'll be lost for the remainder of the lecture.

Don't let your notes cool off. When the lecture is over, spend a minute or two looking over what you've written to be sure it makes sense. Fill in the blank spaces, complete the fragmented ideas, and, if you can, write a one- or two-sentence summary of the main points. Cold notes—notes with isolated words or figures that don't mean anything to you weeks later—aren't much help at exam time.

Q. Help! I need to get organized! How should I manage my time?

A. At the outset, there are two conditions you must recognize. First, there are only 24 hours in the day, whether you sleep or not, and therefore it's only possible to do so much. Second, each of us is geared differently; what works for one student won't necessarily work for another.

Let's take the second point first. During my freshman and sophomore years, I shared a room with a guy whose study habits were atrocious. He drank too much and didn't attend class nearly enough. In some courses he would skip the readings entirely until the night before the final exam. Then he would crack open the textbook—and a bottle of Scotch—and cram all night, usually finishing the book and the Scotch at about the same time. At dawn, he would shave, shower, stride confidently across the campus, and proceed to rack up an A on the final exam. He was graduated cum laude and has had a brilliant career since.

Of course, this guy has a genius-level IQ and a memory like a sponge. He did all the wrong things as a student, and yet he was successful. There are people like that. Unfortunately, I'm not one of them, and it's possible you aren't either. This means we must scramble and plan and plug away for what we get. My roomie was a marvel; I could envy his style, but I would have fallen on my face, literally and academically, if I had attempted to copy it.

Once you've dealt with and accepted your limitations, you can go on from there and try to get a handle on those 24 hours, organizing them into some kind of workable schedule that suits *you.* It shouldn't be the schedule your roommate or friend across the hall follows; it should be yours. One thing is clear, however; you *will* need a schedule to cope with all that needs to be done.

What frequently happens is this: During the first few days of the semester you hit upon the marvelous discovery that college isn't like high school at all. The professor issues an assignment but doesn't check at the next class period to see if you've actually done it or even if you've *begun* to work on a major paper that's due in two weeks. The freedom is wonderful! This means that when you settle down to study and a friend comes in and says, "Let's go see *Gone with the Wind* at the Golden Oldie Theatre tonight," you can put off reading that chapter in American history because it'll keep until tomorrow. But . . . tomorrow comes and now you have two assignments to do. Then— zap! Your first exams are upon you and you still haven't even read the mate- rial, much less organized and reviewed it. How can you avoid panic? Maybe you can't. But *don't* be like Scarlett O'Hara ("I'll think about that tomorrow."). Tomorrow may be too late.

Right away, get a large desk calendar, the kind with a generous square of space for each day, and from every class syllabus write down the dates of labs, exams, paper deadlines, and special activities; also fill in weekends you plan to go home, holidays, your job schedule, all your fixed commit- ments. The calendar alone will tell you a great deal about the peak times and slack times ahead.

You will discover that some classes need systematic attention. In math, accounting, and foreign languages, for example, the material is presented to you in steady doses. You learn one or two new things each day and build on them, which means you need to study on a regular basis. In other classes, in literature and history, for example, the effort may be required in big chunks that must be anticipated well in advance. The calendar will show you at a glance when substantial blocks of time are available for working on these courses.

Next, on a separate sheet of paper, you may want to plan your efforts for an entire week. Schedule in class time, work time, study and research time, and even the periods you need to set aside to review lecture notes and prepare for specific class meetings. (See the examples on pp. 44–45.)

This is a very effective approach, but some students may be overwhelmed by it. They take one look at the filled-in spaces on their time chart, throw up their hands, and shout, "I can't possibly do all that!" or "I just sentenced myself to prison!" And, realistically speaking, maybe for those people the method used by Alcoholics Anonymous works better—one day at a time. Make a list of things to do each day, and don't go to bed until you've done them. For example:

- Study for French test tomorrow.
- Go to library. Work on bibliography for English paper.
- Borrow notes for the biology class I missed when I had the flu.
- Work this afternoon, 1–3:30.
- Read American history chapter for tomorrow.
- Write home.
- Call about ride home for next weekend.

As a general rule, it's best not to think of the total load. If you dwell on how much you have to do, the weight of your burden may become unbearable. Concentrate on short-term objectives—building blocks—that will eventually get you where you're going. By just whacking away steadily and using your spare time wisely, you'll find it somehow will all get done. Or if it doesn't, before long there'll be a new semester and you can start all over again!

Q What's the difference between research and plagiarism?

A Plagiarism is the passing off of someone else's work as your own—the use of ideas without acknowledgment. College professors, you'll find, react angrily to students who plagiarize, so if you're caught, you can, at a minimum, expect to be hit with a grade of F on the assignment. It's also entirely possible you'll be given a failing grade for the entire course. In some

Continued on p. 46

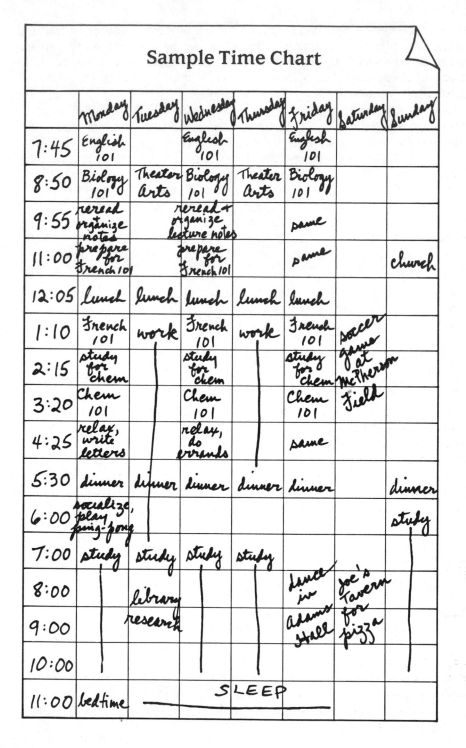

Sample Time Chart

	Monday	Tuesday	Wednesday	Thursday	Friday	Saturday	Sunday
7:45	English 101		English 101		English 101		
8:50	Biology 101	Theater Arts	Biology 101	Theater Arts	Biology 101		
9:55	reread organize notes		reread + organize lecture notes		same		
11:00	prepare for French 101		prepare for French 101		same		church
12:05	lunch	lunch	lunch	lunch	lunch		
1:10	French 101	work	French 101	work	French 101	soccer game at McPherson Field	
2:15	study for chem		study for chem		study for chem		
3:20	Chem 101		Chem 101		Chem 101		
4:25	relax, write letters		relax, do errands		same		
5:30	dinner	dinner	dinner	dinner	dinner		dinner
6:00	socialize, play ping-pong						study
7:00	study	study	study	study			
8:00		library research			dance in Adams Hall	Joe's Tavern for pizza	
9:00							
10:00							
11:00	bedtime		SLEEP				

Your Time Chart

Days ▶ Times ▼							

cases, the professor will instigate proceedings that could even get you expelled and/or keep you out of graduate or professional school.

So be very careful to cite the sources of the ideas and passages you include in your essays and research papers. You will, of course, continually need to consult and use the work of others (that's why there are libraries!); just make certain you don't pretend their work is your own. Bear in mind that your professor (1) reads widely in the field, (2) has a long memory, especially where research is concerned, and (3) can be relentless in the pursuit of plagiarists. You may be tempted late at night, when you find ten beautiful pages in a scholarly book that are made to order for your term paper that's due tomorrow morning, but don't give in.

Q How widespread is cheating?

 On some campuses, it's estimated that 30 to 40 percent of the students at one time or another are guilty of cheating on exams and papers. That's a higher percentage than during the sixties but—are you ready for this?—far lower than back in the Roaring Twenties, when surveys suggested that 70 percent or more of the students were cheating, if only occasionally.

In addition to plagiarism, discussed previously, some of the more common forms of cheating include:

- stealing a copy of the exam ahead of time
- copying from someone else's paper
- sending or receiving signals during a test
- turning in a paper that's been purchased from a commercial research firm (also known as a "term paper mill")
- using unauthorized notes during a test
- taking an exam for another student or letting another student take an exam for you

Sleazy practices all, but unfortunately more or less commonplace on too many campuses. Why? Pressure for good grades is the reason most frequently given. The dog-eat-dog competition for top grades has gotten out of hand at some schools and in some academic disciplines, and it brings out the worst in people. Other contributing factors include stress, permissiveness, and to a large extent, poor management by the institutions themselves. In far too many cases, we professors don't emphasize personal integrity enough, nor do we crack down on cheaters when we do catch them or establish a classroom environment that discourages cheating.

There are exceptions, of course. A number of schools have honor codes, rigidly administered by students themselves, to discourage cheaters. At other schools, such as the University of Maryland, faculty and administrators have dramatically reduced cheating by imposing tougher monitoring standards.

No matter what the atmosphere happens to be on your campus, however, and no matter what other students are doing or what competitive pressures you feel, you don't really gain anything by cheating. If you're caught, you could be suspended or expelled and stuck with a blemish on your record that will follow you for years to come (as more than one candidate for high national office has been embarrassed to discover). No grade is worth that. Even if you're not caught, you still pay a price in terms of guilt and the nagging feeling that you've shortchanged your fellow students and demeaned yourself. No grade is worth that either.

Q. What should I know in order to use the library effectively?

Just a couple of things, actually. First of all, realize that the information you need probably *is* in the library and that you can find it if you know where and how to look. The library is the heart of any campus, and most college libraries have the materials you need to see you through your undergraduate career, hidden though they sometimes may be. I can't emphasize enough how terribly important it is to your education to be able to mobilize the library's resources in your behalf.

During your first few days on campus, allow yourself time for a thorough examination of the main library. Many schools offer group tours for new students. If yours doesn't, simply walk around to the various sections of the library (Serials, Reference, Documents, etc.) and ask one of the librarians in each department to explain briefly how that department operates. Most librarians, despite their snippy image, are good-humored, genuinely caring individuals who are glad to help. At a minimum, you should come away from your initial library orientation with an understanding of the card catalog, which is the key to the library's resources, and you should be familiar with a number of specialized terms:

- Stacks (how they're organized; who can use them and when)
- Library of Congress numbering system

- Dewey Decimal system
- Microfilm, microfiche, microcard (where they are and how to use them)
- Interlibrary loan
- Serials
- Computer search information retrieval systems

The library will probably have an orientation booklet explaining much of this. If so, study it carefully for the shortcuts it offers.

TEST YOURSELF

Ready for a scrimmage? Then consider the following ten questions—a sample of the kind of thing that could send you racing through the library as you work on essays and term papers in the years ahead. Your task is to determine where to *begin* looking for answers to the following.

1. When Charles Portis's third novel, *The Dog of the South,* appeared in 1979, how did the critics react to it?
2. What were the main points in President John F. Kennedy's inaugural address?
3. What articles have appeared in recent years on the subject of acid rain?
4. What are the names and locations of some restaurants in Rochester, New York?
5. W. O. McGeehan has been called "the greatest sportswriter of this century." What were the highlights of his illustrious career?
6. What is the average family income in Huntington, West Virginia? What are the major stores and shopping centers there?
7. What articles and books, if any, has your college president written? What teaching positions has he or she held?
8. What is the exact wording of your state's law regarding the minimum drinking age? What are the penalties for violations?
9. What books does your college library have about Winston Churchill?
10. Name the films that John Huston directed after *The Maltese Falcon.*

Answers. (Note: Information is packaged in many ways, as resourceful librarians know, and the answers to these questions could be found in various places. In each case, I list just one or two sources that will get the job done, but there will undoubtedly be others available to you as well.)

1. First try the *Book Review Digest,* an annual publication that summarizes reviews of important books.
2. The *New York Times* will have carried the full text. Use the *Times Index* for 1961 to pinpoint the edition date and page number, then locate the speech itself in the *Times* file, which your library probably has on microfilm. President Kennedy's speeches are also printed in

the *Public Papers of the President* series, which the documents librarian can make available to you.

3. The *Reader's Guide to Periodical Literature,* a source with which you should become thoroughly familiar, is an excellent place to start. The *Public Affairs Information Service* is also useful for researching this kind of subject.

4. The maps department of the library should have several current U.S. travel/vacation guides on hand. Also, there's a collection of telephone directories, which may include Rochester's yellow pages, in the library someplace, probably in or near the reference department.

5. A brief but authoritative profile of McGeehan is included in the *Dictionary of American Biography.*

6. *Sales and Marketing Management* magazine publishes an annual survey of buying power that describes in detail local economic situations throughout the country. *Editor & Publisher Market Guide* lists principal retail outlets in cities and towns. These volumes are normally shelved in the business department of the library.

7. The *Directory of American Scholars* provides brief biographical sketches of many professors, as does *Who's Who in Higher Education.*

8. A complete collection of your state's statutes is probably shelved in the government documents department.

9. Check the subject index of the card catalog.

10. Mr. Huston's career is profiled in *Halliwell's Filmgoer's Companion* and the *Oxford Companion to Film,* among other sources in the reference department.

How well did you do? This is a no-lose test, so if you scored poorly don't worry about it, at least not yet. Just remind yourself that you and your campus library urgently need to become better acquainted. A little thoughtful effort on your part can reveal to you how to make your library a valuable ally, one that will help you many times during your college years and beyond.

Q What kinds of tests can I expect?

A In huge lecture courses, you'll probably get "objective" tests, which typically include true-or-false questions, matching, multiple choice, identifications, and completions. These are more convenient to grade and are often handled by machines or teaching assistants. In smaller classes, particularly those in which discussion is encouraged, you're more likely to get essay exams, which provide practice in organizing concepts and writing.

Q How often will I be tested?

A At a minimum you should expect a midterm exam, which is usually administered at a regular class meeting, and a final, which is scheduled during a special exam period at the end of the term. A final exam normally lasts 2 or 3 hours, though you may well finish in less time. In some classes, especially those in which new terms and concepts are continually being introduced, you may be tested as frequently as once a week.

Q How should I prepare for "objective" tests?

A An "objective" test is one that deals with hard information more than ideas. True-or-false, multiple-choice, matching questions—these are the kinds of things you can expect if the professor announces that the test will be "objective."

Any test is a less-than-perfect instrument for measuring student progress. Each semester some of the ablest students, young men and women who think clearly, write and talk well, and work hard on the subject material, fail to come through exams with the superlative grades they deserve. Perhaps they suffer from what educational psychologists call "test anxiety." I'm told that some 25 percent of all students are affected by test anxiety, often to a considerable degree. The numbers are believed to be even higher for minority students. For whatever reason, some good students just don't test well. Others, however, seem to outdo themselves, to perform above their capabilities during exams. These individuals may not be brilliant, but they are shrewd enough to squeeze the full mileage out of the knowledge they do possess. Also, they take everything they're given, and sometimes professors give away quite a bit. Most professors have never taken Tests and Measurements, Educational Psychology, or other courses in teaching methods and techniques. Partly as a result, we often goof up on our own exams, unintentionally dropping hints for those students clever enough to take advantage of them.

For instance, this question might show up on an American history exam:

At the outset of World War II, the President of the United States was:
A. Harry S Truman
B. Dwight D. Eisenhower
C. Franklin D. Roosevelt
D. Herbert C. Hoover

Okay. Assume you were stumped by that one. Later in the same test, however, you find:

During the early days of World War II, President Roosevelt's Secretary of State was:
A. Henry Wallace
B. Cordell Hull
C. George C. Marshall
D. Douglas MacArthur

Well, you may not know who the Secretary of State was (Mr. Hull), but you would have to be pretty unobservant not to have noticed that the second question provides the answer to the first. I've left myself open to just this kind of thing many times and I'm amazed at how few students have grabbed the freebies that have been available to them. If you really *study* the test you can pick up clues that add points to your score. Here are some other tips:

Don't leave anything blank. You have a shot at points if you make a stab at an answer, and you sure won't get any if you leave the item untouched. On true-or-false questions you have a fifty-fifty chance of hitting, and on a multiple-choice question your odds are usually no worse than one in four. On short-answer completions, a prof may give you a point or two for making the effort, even if your answer is almost entirely wrong. (Warning: Some professors penalize their students for guessing, so be sure to find out what your instructor's policy is beforehand.)

Don't overkill. Suppose you're asked to identify the term "rationalism." Each identification is worth, say, 5 points and should be answered briefly. You happen to have studied the dickens out of rationalism and so you're tempted to write three full pages on the subject. Don't. You'll get only 5 points, tops, on this one, no matter how much you write, so answer the question swiftly and move on. The shrewdest test takers are ruthless in allocating their time. They demolish the easy stuff quickly and efficiently, stockpiling those precious minutes for use on the really tough questions that carry big point values.

Know the professor's objectives for each test. If you can get your prof to say, for example, something like "I'm primarily interested in checking on how well you understand basic terminology at this point," you can prepare accordingly.

The best remedy for test anxiety is simply to study the material thoroughly during the semester. When exam time comes, you'll probably get lucky. As a highly successful football coach is fond of saying, "The harder I work, the luckier I get."

How should I prepare for essay exams?

The essay exam, some professors assert, calls for a higher order of mental processes. Instead of merely recognizing material, as in objective tests, you must also be prepared to organize it, evaluate it, argue with it, generalize and particularize from it, and relate it to other situations. If an objective test calls for knowledge, then an essay exam calls for knowledge, judgment, and skill. Your judgment will be demonstrated by the way you organize your thoughts (by what you use and what you leave out) and your skill by how well you present what you know.

An example: Suppose that your professor for Introduction to Sociology concludes a unit on the subject of advertising with this essay question:

> Support or refute this statement: "Advertising causes people to buy things they don't need with money they don't have to impress neighbors they don't know."

Your approach? First consider the teacher's objective, which is probably to find out how familiar you are with the effects of advertising on society. You might then outline your answer in the following way:

I. Advertising critics make these points:
   A. Advertising is wasteful and expensive.
   B. Much advertising is in poor taste.
   C. Advertising can foster materialism and a false set of values, especially among children.
   D. Some advertising is misleading in that it seems to promise instant cures for all problems, both personal and social.
II. On the other hand, supporters of advertising claim the following:
   A. By stimulating demand, advertising speeds up the marketing process and can actually result in the lowering of some prices.

B. Advertising supports the media of mass communications; without advertising, newspapers, radio, and television might have to be financed—and therefore controlled—by the government.

C. Advertising fulfills a massive educational function, teaching us about new products and services, helping us spend our money wisely.

III. But if advertising is out of control, who should regulate it?

A. The government. (But could this lead to censorship and thought control?)

B. The industry itself. (But how effective is industry self-regulation?)

C. The public, through education. (But this is slow and uncertain.)

D. Possibly a combination of all of the above.

IV. Conclusion.

It probably won't matter much which you do, praise advertising or bury it, for there is no simple solution. Your professor will be more interested in seeing how well you understand all sides of the issue and how skillfully and persuasively you present your case.

In preparing for an essay exam, then, you'll need to search through the material for major themes you can pull together into convincing arguments. Just because a topic is broad, however, doesn't mean your approach can be vague. There's a difference. In essay exams, as a general guide, the more specific your points, the more credible your case.

Q What if I HAVE to cram all night?

A At some point during your college career, you will have to study into the wee hours of the morning, or at least you'll think you have to. And despite what other students may tell you, there really is no magic formula that's guaranteed to keep you awake and productive while you're pulling an all-nighter. (Tiny catnaps, for example, may refresh you, but they may also zonk you out for the duration, depending on your individual constitution. Caffeine pills work well for some students and give others the jitters.)

Your best bet, easier said than done, is to convince yourself that the work ahead is necessary and important and then get in there and do it. A surgeon, called to the hospital at midnight, knowing he'll work until dawn sewing up victims of an accident and then see patients in his office all the following day, simply grits his teeth and does his job.

You might be able to help yourself by loading up on food (the sugar and the protein may restore your energy). Coffee, tea, and cola might perk you up, but don't overindulge, because ingesting too much caffeine can be counterproductive. It's also a good idea to take an occasional break for a cold shower, a brisk walk in the fresh air, or maybe some calisthenics. If you're going to need blue books, make sure you get them well in advance; you don't want the distraction of having to chase over to the bookstore on the way to the exam. (A blue book is an inexpensive writing tablet professors often require you to use when taking an essay exam.)

Avoid speed and other controlled substances at all costs. These stimulants may well get you through the night, but you'll be so looped the next day you won't be able to think straight during the exam.

While you're studying, make sure that you cover *all* of the assigned material, even if you're only skimming. Given the choice of studying half the material thoroughly or all of it superficially, opt for the latter. Even a fleeting familiarity with some chapters of a textbook may be enough to allow you to wing it through part of an essay exam. Study the table of contents to see how the material is organized and presented, then methodically divide the material into blocks and decide how much time you can afford to spend on each unit. Allow for some time at the end to compose yourself, to do a quick review, and to stroll unhurriedly to the exam. You'll want your brain to be as clear as it can be under the circumstances in order to be able to focus on the task ahead.

Q How do I pick a topic for my term paper?

A You'll find that your college professors give you a great deal of freedom to research and write about subjects of your own choosing. Whenever possible, try to use this freedom to select an area you are personally interested in; if you're bored with the subject, you'll almost certainly bore your reader—the professor—as well. Also make sure your topic is manageable—that is, narrow enough for you to handle—and that it is an issue for which you can present conclusions rather than simply report facts.

Suppose, for example, you have to write a term paper for your U.S. history course, and you've made a preliminary decision to write about the Civil War period. You're not particularly interested in military strategy or the economic implications of the war; you are, however, interested in public opinion and attitude formation, behavior patterns, and press coverage.

At the outset, give yourself a good soaking in the literature. Examine books dealing with the Civil War in general, but look for what the authors say about newspaper accounts of the fighting. You don't have to read each book in its entirety; use that wonderful invention, the index, to zero in swiftly on the passages you need.

Once you've completed a survey of the literature, it's time to begin narrowing the topic into something that can be done, and done by you, within reasonable limits. "How the Press Covered the Civil War," for example, is not workable. "How the Confederate Press Covered the Civil War" is better; you've cut the topic in half, but you're still stuck with lots of newspapers and lots of battles and more research than you can possibly handle. While you continue to tighten your focus, check on the library's holdings of old newspaper files and find out what's there for you to work with. Eventually you might come up with a question: How did two influential newspapers, one northern and one southern, report one battle?—and, *voila!* a topic: "Triumph or Tragedy? Comparative Press Accounts of the Firing on Fort Sumter." Properly done, this has the makings of a useful case study in public opinion, propaganda, and the reaction of the press and the public to a significant news event. It's rather less grand than "How the Press Covered the Civil War," but it's a topic you can deal with. Equally important, it will let you show off your critical skills—your ability to analyze, compare, contrast, and generalize. In other words, not only will you describe a situation, you will be able to draw conclusions from it and suggest its larger context. That's the kind of intellectual workout that will do you good—and it won't hurt your grade any, either.

Q How can I improve my reading skills?

A "Fifty percent of effective reading comes in learning how to get organized for the reading task ahead," the director of a college counseling center reports. "We can teach that. Twenty-five percent is in motivation. We can't teach that. The other twenty-five percent is what the student is born with."

Until now, your reading skills may never have been truly tested. In high school, the learning comes largely through listening, but in college the emphasis will shift. During your first week of classes, your professors order, "Start reading!" Some students aren't able, without help, to respond. A few can barely read at all. Many others lack the vocabulary and technique to read at the brisk tempo their college courses will require.

Fortunately, almost every campus has a learning skills center, operated by the counseling office or, perhaps, by the school of education, to offer remedial assistance free of charge to students who need it. Qualified counselors employ a variety of approaches, ranging from individual tutorials to reading workshops to noncredit classes that may last several months. The techniques of speed reading may be taught, not to turn the student into a whiz capable of devouring hundreds of pages an hour, but to develop a mind-set for managing a reading assignment and tackling it with confidence.

Few students are ever required to avail themselves of services provided by a learning skills center. Participation is purely voluntary, and how much you improve depends to an overwhelming extent on your own determination. For those students who do decide to attack their reading problems, the improvement usually is dramatic.

If you don't need remedial work, learning how to read effectively then becomes a matter of sorting out the material and bearing down hard until you understand it. Begin by examining how the chapter is organized. Before you dig into the actual text, look over the titles and subheadings to see how the author has outlined the presentation. (And it *has* been outlined: major points, supporting information, conclusions.) Seek out the author's wavelength, as reflected in style, approach, teaching objectives.

Communication is normally a matter of getting two minds to share the same thought. In this situation, though, you're looking for *three-way* communication among your professor, the author of the book you're reading, and yourself. So after you've finished reading the assignment, ask yourself these questions about it: Why did the professor want us to read this material? What was the author trying to explain? How was the piece developed? What were the key points? Do I understand each of the main points? Each concept? Each term? What test questions might the professor ask about this material? How would I organize my answers to them? How does this piece fit in with the other material covered in lectures and readings?

Finally, you might try explaining what you've read, as if you're trying to educate a friend. After all, as many a professor will readily admit, the best way to learn a subject is to teach it.

Q How can I improve my writing skills?

 "There's nothing to writing," the famous newspaperman Red Smith once said. "All you have to do is sit down at a typewriter and open up a vein." For many college students, writing is an incredibly painful experience. Many try to avoid writing whenever possible. It's a mistake to do so, however, for writing is almost certainly the most important factor in determining academic success. Top writers get top grades, mediocre writers get mediocre grades, and bad writers—those who are unable to achieve a minimal level of competence—are likely to find themselves flirting with academic probation or suspension.

By "good writing," I don't mean literature on the order of a John Steinbeck or an Ernest Hemingway; I mean writing that explains ideas clearly and logically and in passable English. In college, your writing will be tested again and again, most commonly in essay examinations and research papers. While grading these efforts, your professor will evaluate presentation as well as content, in other words, not only what you write, but the clarity and skill with which you write it.

Most colleges offer full-length courses devoted to the improvement of writing skills, and you may want to take one or more of them. In the meantime, these pointers might help:

Make an outline. This is positively essential for organizing your thoughts and developing them clearly. (Don't make the mistake of assuming that a written outline is mere junior high school stuff; I've seen prizewinning professional journalists prepare an outline before writing a straight news story.) You should whip up an outline before you tackle an essay exam, even though an outline will take a precious few minutes and you desperately need the time. Your essay will be clearer, more persuasive, and certainly more polished if you outline it first.

Eliminate the mechanical errors. This requires catching and correcting all the mistakes in grammar, spelling, punctuation, and so on. Many professors simply cannot bring themselves to award a high grade to a student whose writing is mechanically flawed. Some academic hard-liners will even flunk an otherwise brilliant essay if it contains a number of misspelled words. Lug a pocket dictionary to class with you, if necessary, and challenge yourself on the spelling of any word you aren't sure of; efforts to improve the mechanics of your writing will pay off handsomely.

Revise and rewrite. No matter how good you think your first draft is, a careful revision of your out-of-class essay will surely be better. Many good writers will do four or five revisions, sometimes more, before they think a piece is ready to go. "That spontaneous wit I'm supposedly famous for," a noted author admitted not long ago, "usually comes on about the fifth draft." The weakest student papers I see are those that are obviously first drafts, rough and hurried ones at that.

Remember that neatness counts. Type if you possibly can. (You may have no choice; some professors won't accept handwritten papers.) Teachers may not admit it, but we are favorably impressed with papers that are neat and legible, just as we are put off by papers that are messy and disorganized. If you don't take pride in your work, the professor won't think much of it either.

Use the terminology of the course. Many teachers like it when you demonstrate a familiarity with the specialized language of the field. This suggests that you are beginning to involve yourself with the course, and it results in a sense of gratification on the part of the professor and more points for you.

Go the distance. Write as much as your professor permits. If the assignment calls for an eight-page paper, don't hand in three pages and say, "I thought you would respond better to three really good pages than eight pages filled with hot air." Not likely. Remember, your teacher has to have some basis for evaluation, and he or she can't give you a grade for work that isn't there. Follow the same dogged reasoning on your essay exams. Don't expect a top grade on a brief essay. Write until you have to quit. Many professors will judge you on quantity as well as quality, so get your money's worth. There's an old saying about some profs: They don't really read the essay exams, they just weigh them, and the heaviest papers get the best grades.

Q What will I need to know about computers?

 The computer invasion hit campuses in the sixties. Students made jokes about it, but faculty members, many of us, were terrified. "What are we going to do?" a history professor worried aloud at lunch one day. "The computer represents all that I oppose about modern society. The computer is cold, impersonal, relentless. And besides," he admitted, finally, "I don't understand how the damned thing works."

"You'd better learn," said someone else at the table. "The rumor is that we're going to use the computer to handle registration next semester. Students will input their course requests and the computer will assign classes, sections, times—the whole business."

It was, we decided, a dark hour for higher education.

At that moment, the registrar strode into the faculty dining room and took a chair at our table. He was expecting a quiet, congenial lunch; what he got instead was a sudden, hostile barrage of questions about the computer, that menace that threatened the academic world as we knew it.

"Now wait a minute, people, wait a minute!" he protested, laughing. "You guys worry too much. The computer is just a clerk. It just does what we tell it. The computer is nothing more than a big, fat, stupid clerk."

"Good grief," moaned Fred, from the English department. "Not another one of those in the registrar's office!"

In the years since, of course, computers have come to permeate virtually every office on the campus, even Fred's English department, where computers are now utilized on tasks ranging from word processing of faculty manuscripts to a content analysis of Shakespeare's plays.

There's no doubt that you will need a computer at various times throughout your college years. Maybe it will only be to run an occasional high-speed search for information at the library, but you'll probably find far more uses for computers than this. Not to worry, though. Most of your college's computers will be "user friendly," that is, their programs will take little time to learn, and they will protect you from making ghastly mistakes.

On many campuses, including Harvard, at least one course in computer science is required of all students, and a number of colleges are actually providing each student with his or her own individual computer terminal. Virtually all campuses today are equipped with computer labs for student use; indeed, many colleges and universities now routinely assign a minimum of one computer-related exercise per semester in many of the courses throughout the curriculum.

Whether you're forced to or not, however, you're well advised to become computer literate as soon as possible. Ideally, you'll also pick up some additional math (math requirements in the future will inevitably become stiffer). If you can learn a little something about programming, then so much the better; BASIC—Beginner's All-purpose Symbolic Instruction Code—is a popular language to start with.

No matter what you do, develop your typing skills. When you're seated in front of a computer terminal you'll have enough on your mind without the added bother of figuring out where the letters and numbers are on what is, essentially, a typewriter keyboard.

Q Why should I be required to study a foreign language? Doesn't most of the world speak English?

A English has indeed become enormously popular around the globe in recent years. It's now estimated that more than 414 million people speak English. A whopping figure—until you realize that the other 90 percent of the world's peoples speak something else.

Americans tend to adopt an imperious attitude toward language, expecting everybody else to learn ours and spare us from having to learn theirs. Even colleges and universities, supposedly islands of understanding in a sea of chaos, are frequently ambivalent about foreign language. Most of the students in arts and sciences who are required to enroll in foreign language courses do so with gritted teeth. An advisee of mine offered a typical response. "I don't want to be an interpreter or a translator or a foreign language teacher," she complained. "So what other reason could there possibly be to study a foreign language?"

There are plenty of reasons, of course, especially for students who are able to combine their language skills with something else. An excellent booklet, "Foreign Languages and Careers," (available from the Modern Language Association, 62 Fifth Avenue, New York, New York 10011), puts it this way:

> Today's job market is difficult. Employers can afford to be highly selective, and an extra skill often makes the difference. A good engineer who speaks German is more likely to be hired by a Swiss firm's American branch than an engineer with equivalent qualifications who speaks nothing but English. A sales manager who knows Portuguese has a better chance of getting a higher-paid assignment in Brazil than one who doesn't.

The booklet's authors, Lucille J. Honig and Richard I. Brod, outline career opportunities for language graduates in a wide range of fields: business, industry, science, education, international law, health services, social work, the missionary and religious fields, travel and tourism, and a good many others. The possibilities are there and they are exciting. Ironically, however, fewer high school and college students enroll in foreign language courses now than a decade ago. Less than 4 percent of those who are graduated from a public high school have had more than two years of a foreign language. Compared with other countries, our national track record in mastering languages other than our own is pretty dismal, and the price we are paying in terms of lost political, social, and commercial opportunities is a dreadfully high one.

In some parts of the United States a person now needs to show proficiency in Spanish to qualify for a job as a policeman, social worker, or journalist. (We are now the fourth-largest Spanish-speaking nation in the world.) The huge influx of tourists from overseas has literally forced business executives to seek out new employees who have foreign language skills. International marketing departments of many corporations are expanding dramatically.

Job implications aside, there are other reasons to learn a second or third language. Consider the following, a graceful and persuasive passage that concludes "Foreign Languages and Careers."

> Language study is pleasurable and valuable in itself because it furnishes the key to thinking patterns, culture, and social institutions of a foreign nation or nations; because it affords insights into the nature of language itself and the human mind; because it fosters a sense of shared humanity among persons who have learned to break down the barriers that im-

pede communications. In addition, language expands and enhances the pleasures of travel, of good literature and the arts, and of social interaction. By combining career aspirations and the humanizing and broadening aspects of the study of foreign language and culture, one can make a sound investment in a stimulating and rewarding future.

Q Why should I have to take so many liberal arts courses?

A A few years ago, when I was chairman of an academic department at a southern university, the staff and I traced the careers of the department's several hundred former students. We found an astonishing number in positions of leadership, including more than one third who were holding down the top job wherever they happened to be. That little survey convinced me, if I had ever had any doubt, that we are in the business of helping educate young men and women who will one day make a difference in their chosen fields, who will, in William Faulkner's phrase, "not only endure, but prevail."

The liberal arts courses you're facing now may not help much when you tackle your first, entry-level job after graduation. They can, however, help give you the scope and depth and attitude of mind you'll need later on. A statement in the 1982 *Bulletin of Yale University* says it well:

> In our complex society and rapidly changing world, a sound education must prepare students for an unpredictable future, not merely by preparing them for particular careers, but by teaching them how to learn. Yale's purpose is thus a manifold one. At one level, it is to develop in its students the abilities they need to contribute to society. At a deeper level, it is to be sure that those abilities are rooted in an education which is sufficiently substantial and flexible to enable its students to deal with the unexpected turns their society will take. At its most fundamental level, however, Yale's purpose is to nourish in its students the motivation and affection for learning which will lead them to continue to develop their intellectual, creative, and moral capacities throughout the whole of their lives.

You could delete the word "Yale" from that passage, substitute the name of your own college or university, and get a pretty clear idea of why those liberal arts courses are required of you. Herman B. Wells, the legendary president of Indiana University, once testified before a committee of the state legislature in behalf of his school's proposed budget. One of the lawmakers objected to the appropriation to pay for "all those liberal arts courses." "I don't want to be associated with any university," Wells is said to have replied, "that trains people to live and work throughout their lives without once asking why." He got his appropriation.

Q What is a pass-fail option?

A It's a plan through which you can explore an unfamiliar area of study without fracturing your grade average in the process. For example, Albert, a premed student, usually carries a course schedule heavy in such subjects as biology and chemistry. This semester, however, he has, for a change, some flexibility in selecting his classes. Poring eagerly over the course catalog, he spies what appears to be a marvelous elective: English 337, The Modern American Novel. "Wonderful!" the creative spirit in him exclaims. 'Fitzgerald! Hemingway! Faulkner! I've always wanted to study them. This is just the change I need!"

"Better hold off a sec, buddy," warns the premed side of him. "American lit could be dangerous territory for someone with your science orientation. That class you're so eager for will be wall-to-wall English majors—literary sharks—and they'll snap up all the top grades. You may be in over your head, and that C minus or D won't look so hot on the old transcript, will it?" Albert is in a quandary.

His solution? Sign up for the course anyway, but do so on a pass-fail basis. Terms of this option differ from one campus to another (as does the name; sometimes it's called "pass–no pass" or "credit only"), but essentially the option permits you to earn credit hours for a course without having the grade figured into your overall average or even recorded on your transcript. Thus Albert can take The Modern American Novel, and no one will ever know what his grade was; it could range from an A plus to a D minus, just as long as he passes.

The option usually has some restrictions. It may be used only for electives, not required courses; you must be in good academic standing and not on probation; and normally you won't be permitted to take more than a total of about four courses on a pass-fail basis. Your professor's approval is normally not required; in fact, he or she isn't even supposed to know which students in the class are taking the course pass-fail.

Q What are repeat options?

A Suppose you do poorly in a course: You get an F, a D, or even a C. Suppose further that you're distressed about the effect this grade will have on your cumulative GPA or on a prospective employer or a graduate school admissions officer. Or suppose you simply feel you didn't understand the course, and you really want to or need to for another course you're planning to take. It's entirely possible that your college has a provision that allows you to take the course again. If you do exercise your repeat option, then only the second grade is used when your grade point average is computed.

The repeat option can be useful for students who are desperate to attain a certain GPA, those shooting for Phi Beta Kappa, for example, or those who must somehow pull up to a 2.0 to spring loose from academic probation. Other students might use a repeat option simply to neutralize a disappointing performance and prove that they can earn a top grade in a particular subject.

Often a school will limit the number of repeat options to a maximum of three or four. You may also be required to notify your dean in writing when you use one of your repeat options, so make sure your faculty adviser and dean know what you're doing.

Q How do I determine my grade point average?

A Grade points are used to translate letter grades into numerical values; they represent a more precise and uniform way of measuring your academic performance. On most campuses, grade points, or quality points, as they're sometimes called, are awarded this way:

> A = 4 grade points per semester hour
> B = 3 grade points per semester hour
> C = 2 grade points per semester hour
> D = 1 grade point per semester hour
> F = 0 grade points

Each course, as you know by now, is worth a specified number of college credits, normally called semester hours (or quarter hours, if your school is on the quarter system). Your English 101 course, for example, is probably a 3-hour course, a course carrying 3 semester hours of credit. If you made a C in it, multiply the grade points given for a C (2 for each credit hour) times the number of credit hours (in this case, 3). Do that for each course in your schedule, and you can compute your semester GPA. Here's an example:

Course name	Credits	Grade	Grade Points
English	3	C	3 credits x 2 points = 6
French	3	B	3 credits x 3 points = 9
Biology	4	C	4 credits x 2 points = 8
Art History	2	A	2 credits x 4 points = 8
Sociology	3	B	3 credits x 3 points = 9
Archery	1	P	————
	16		40

(Note: No grade point is given for the Pass you got in archery. You earned 16 credit hours toward graduation, which is the main thing, but since the archery credit was not taken for a grade we will use only 15 here for purposes of computing your GPA.)

Divide the 40 grade points by the 15 credit hours:

$$40 \div 15 = 2.67 \text{ (grade point average)}$$

This means you have an average of C plus or, as you will probably inform your parents, a B minus, for the semester. As the semesters roll by, you build a cumulative GPA (or "cume"), and most students know theirs down to the third or fourth decimal point.

Q How important are grades?

A Very. Grades are the means by which your academic score will be kept. It's a lousy system, and many people place far too much stock in it. I once heard a macho football coach put it to his team this way: "Folks will hand you this garbage," he said, more or less, "about 'it's not whether you win or lose, but how you play the game.' Well, boys, I'm tellin' you this: How you play the game determines whether you win or lose!"

That coach's win-at-any-cost philosophy is abhorrent, but I assure you many share it. Even in the hallowed Halls of Ivy, a distressing number of students believe they aren't "winning" at college unless they have a top GPA to prove it. Many of these students will seek out mediocre but easy professors and enroll in gut courses that aren't helpful but virtually guarantee high marks. They'll fawn over professors, even cheat if necessary, anything and everything to rack up an impressive grade point average.

At the other extreme are those relatively few cavalier students who ignore grades altogether. They may become well educated, but their transcripts can't convince anybody of it.

My advice is, be a "prudent student," one who is conscientious about grades but who has a sense of perspective (and personal values) firmly intact. One thing is certain: You will be asked about grades by parents, the financial aid office, employers, academic and professional societies, graduate and professional schools, scholarship committees, and any number of individuals, including nosy neighbors, pesky brothers and sisters, anxious aunts, and proud grandparents.

Q. If I'm bombing out in a course, can I just take an Incomplete instead and then regroup?

A. An Incomplete is normally granted to a student who is otherwise passing but who cannot, for good reason, finish the work on time. It happens. You may come down with the flu just as you begin to write your term paper. A few colleges seem to allow Incompletes to be given pretty freely. On most campuses, however, you'll need to show that circumstances beyond your control prevented you from meeting your course deadlines. Your professor will determine (1) whether you can and/or should be awarded an Incomplete and (2) if so, just what you must do in order to remove the Incomplete from your transcript and receive a letter grade for the course. In any case, it's up to you to initiate the request for a grade of Incomplete.

An Incomplete may take some pressure off, but in reality it simply postpones the pressure. That term paper will still have to be written, and it will be a monkey on your back until you get it done.

Avoid Incompletes if you can. It's far better to tough it out and finish rather than have a course hanging fire for semesters to come. Your work probably won't get better; as a matter of fact, it will get worse as the material cools off. And you probably don't need the extra burden in any semester of removing Incompletes from the semester before.

If there is a crisis, however, especially near the end of the semester, the Incomplete grade can be a godsend in averting what would otherwise be an academic disaster.

Q. What can I do if I feel I've received an unfair grade?

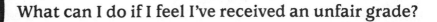

AGrading is the hardest, dreariest part of the teaching profession, and only an arrogant fool would claim that professors don't commit grading mistakes. We on the faculty are misleading our students and ourselves if we pretend that our grading methods are scientific, accurate, perfectly proportioned, and uniformly fair. They're not.

Every professor occasionally misjudges or miscalculates when attempting to arrive at a grade, and if you think you've been unfairly dealt with you should speak up about it. Give the professor a chance to review your work and, if warranted, correct any injustice that may have been done.

If you do have a complaint about a grade, don't pitch a fit about it in class, or even just after class. Avoid forcing your professor into a hurried public decision that almost certainly won't be in your favor. Instead, make an appointment to discuss your grade during the professor's office hours, when you can present your case fully and, you hope, with the professor's undivided attention. Your arguments should be on the merits of the work itself, not merely on the fact that you put in a lot of time working on the assignment. A teacher is not evaluating your life-style, your study habits, or what you intended to write but didn't; he or she merely grades the results of your labors, the paper or test that you actually turned in. Your best approach is not to question the teacher's competence or judgment—presumably these have been verified by others who are in a position to know—but instead to point out things that may have been overlooked or misunderstood. Don't press too hard; professors, like most people, resent being leaned on.

Even if you don't win this particular case, and many professors, once they've determined a grade, are hard to budge, your office visit can have certain strategic value. For one thing, you'll probably learn a great deal about your professor's grading criteria, and that's valuable information to have. Also, your presentation, assuming you handled yourself in an intelligent and mature fashion, may convince the professor that you're a serious, conscientious student. This is a favorable image that may prove decisive if, say, you wind up the semester with a point average that's on the borderline between a B plus and an A minus.

If you feel your grade for the entire course has been unfair, then you certainly have the right to appeal. Present as much supporting evidence as you can: all your previous tests, papers, and other documents. Recall the professor's own ground rules for determining grades (they'll be in your syllabus from the first class meeting) and argue your case accordingly. A well-thought-out, unemotional, courteous presentation is more likely to work. (Some arguments that won't are: "I need a good grade to get into law school" or "I'll lose my eligibility to try out for cheerleader" or "If I don't make at least a C in this course I can't be initiated into my sorority." Again, your professor is paid to evaluate your work in a specific class—not to boost your career or social aspirations.) And don't demand an immediate decision; allow the professor time to review your entire file and to rethink how your performance compared with that of the rest of the class.

If the professor refuses to change your grade and you still feel strongly about it, you can carry your appeal up the line. The system will vary from one campus to the next, so consult your student handbook for specific procedures. Your next step would normally be to arrange a meeting with the department chair, then the dean. On larger campuses, there may be an official ombudsman to handle student grievances.

No matter what procedure is involved, however, most grade appeals fail. They ultimately come down to questions of judgment by the professor who was hired to teach the class. Department chairpeople, deans, and even college presidents are most reluctant to overturn a professor's decision when an individual student's grade is concerned, for they realize that this kind of interference can create severe morale problems throughout the faculty. The real value of your appeal, assuming your complaint is legitimate, is that it will draw attention to your professor's unfairness and/or incompetence—and perhaps cause his or her superiors to begin wondering whether such a person should ultimately be retained. If a number of other students file similar appeals, and if these appeals are valid, the professor's career at the institution will be affected. That won't do you any immediate good, obviously, but there are misfits in teaching, as in anything else, and they should be found out.

Unless your professor is indeed an utter incompetent, or some other kind of menace, however, you're probably better off accepting your grade, even through gritted teeth, and not making a federal case out of it. Commit your energies to a good showing next semester instead. Unless you have a compelling reason, don't waste your time haggling over something in the past. Most probably you and your professor had what's best described as an honest disagreement; you saw your performance one way and the prof saw it another. So you did get a C in a course where you feel you deserved a B. Next time you may luck out with an A when you truly deserved a B or even a C. Life is like that.

I've been told that jogging will improve my grades. Will it?

Not directly. Not unless you jog over to the library and hit the books. Indirectly, however, regular exercise may help by enhancing your stamina and capacity to handle the academic grind. Many professors, while cheerfully admitting they have no proof, believe that there is a positive connection between physical exertion and intellectual performance. One of my colleagues, an obsessive jogger, virtually insists that the advanced students who do research projects with him also maintain individual programs of physical activity. One of his students, stumped by a complex problem in statistical analysis, visited the professor's study to ask for help. "How often do you work out?" demanded the professor in a tone suggesting that strenuous exercise for the body might be the key toward unlocking secrets of the mind.

One of the leading fitness advocates is Kenneth H. Cooper, a physician whose works on aerobics (exercises such as jogging, swimming, running, and cycling that stimulate heart and lung activity) have sold in the millions of copies. Dr. Cooper claims that sustained aerobic exercise will produce a "training effect," which, in his words, "helps your lungs operate more efficiently . . . enlarges your blood vessels, making them more pliable and reduces the resistance to blood flow . . . increases your blood supply, especially the red-blood cells and hemoglobin . . . makes healthier body tissue, supplying it with more oxygen . . . does wonders for your heart, conditioning it as a strong, healthy muscle, relaxed and slow at rest, yet capable of accelerating to much higher work-loads without undue fatigue or strain . . . helps you eat better, digest better, and eliminate wastes better . . . helps you sleep better . . . may even make you feel better, mentally and emotionally."

The crusading Dr. Cooper has many followers, and I confess to being one of them. I jog three or four times a week, 3 or more miles per outing. I can't honestly say that jogging works miracles for me, but I keep plugging away and would miss it if I ever stopped. Perhaps as many as one fourth of my faculty colleagues, and probably a third to one half of my students, are involved in regular exercise programs.

For all its other real and imagined benefits, however, there's still no certainty that exercise leads to improved mental output. The people who excel in the classroom, in other words, do so for reasons other than their exercise programs. So go ahead and jog if you want to and you're medically fit to begin a regimen of strenuous physical exercise, but don't count on jogging in and of itself to propel you onto the Dean's List.

CHAPTER 3

THE PROFS

If you've ever watched one of those old MGM movies in which a college professor character is featured, you've got the stereotype down pat: tweed jacket with leather patches at the elbows; horn-rimmed glasses; all in all, a detached, rather fussy, graying-at-the-temples figure seated in his book-lined study (in coat and tie, of course) absorbed in *The Origin of Species* or some other light reading. A lovely portrait, and one that may even have had some validity to it—fifty years ago.

Today's professors defy typecasting. In appearance, they're as varied as an urban landscape, and their personalities run the gamut from austere to zany. There is one thing professors do have in common, and it may be the only thing: They each worked very hard to win those positions on college and university faculties.

You will respect most of your professors and even adore some of them; a few, for one reason or another, you may come to dread. Your primary concern, however, should not be whether you like the professor, but whether you can learn from him or her. Consider this all-too-familiar refrain, "Well, yes, I did get a D in calculus. I just didn't like my teacher." Sound feeble? It is.

Still, your studies will be easier and far more pleasant if you and your professors are in tune, so it's a wise move on your part, and good personal politics, to find out something about the diverse group of men and women who compose your college faculty.

Q. What if I need to talk to a professor outside the classroom? Is it possible to do so?

A. Sure it is. Professors are expected, and at many schools required, to maintain office hours, a regular time each week when the office door is open and students are welcome to come in for conferences. Most professors genuinely like their students (if we didn't, we wouldn't have gone into teaching in the first place), and we enjoy the informal conversations with them outside the classroom.

This does not mean that your professors will always be readily and casually available. Most of us may be somewhat less than enthusiastic about a student conversation that begins this way, for example: "Hullo, Doc. I was in the building early today. I have a class in 45 minutes and some time to kill, so I thought I'd just drop by and visit. . . ." You wouldn't drop in on your physician or your dentist or lawyer that way; your teacher is a professional whose time is just as important (if not always as expensive) as that of professionals in other areas.

Students who have a reason to talk, however, are always welcome. It doesn't have to be an earthshaking reason, either; sometimes you may need clarification on a paper that's coming due, or you didn't quite understand an idea that was presented in yesterday's lecture. Or maybe you need advice about books to read or courses to take next semester or pointers for finding a summer job. Let your professor help, if at all possible, and, if the problem can't be handled during regular office hours, your prof can usually arrange the time for a specific appointment with you.

Should you phone the professor at home? Some of my colleagues resent it when students do. They argue that professors have the right to a private life when they leave the campus. A surprising number have unlisted numbers, and a few have disconnected their telephones altogether. "What happens if there's an emergency on campus?" I once asked a colleague who'd recently switched to an unlisted home telephone number. "In a well-run university," he replied, sniffing, "there are no emergencies."

There are some nights during the academic year when I know I'll get a number of telephone calls, all from worried students. After the fourth or fifth call my wife will inquire: "Giving an exam tomorrow, are you?" Yes, and the students are calling with questions about the lectures and readings that should have been raised a month ago. There's nothing like an exam or a term paper deadline to blast open the channels of communication between student and professor.

Remember, however, that your professor probably hits the sack far earlier than you do. Though 2 o'clock in the morning may be the merest shank of the evening to you, it is long past your prof's normal bedtime. Whatever academic problem you develop at that hour is best kept until tomorrow.

Q How can my professor justify having a class attendance policy? If I paid my money, isn't it my own business whether or not I attend class?

A The fact that you paid your tuition, for which the school is no doubt grateful, does not give you the right to operate entirely on your own terms as a student. The institution has certain rules, which you agreed to, directly or indirectly, and one of those rules holds that the professor is in charge of his or her class. So long as the professor behaves reasonably, and having an attendance policy certainly is not unreasonable, he or she can lay down and enforce a law that says you must attend class or have your grade affected accordingly.

Attendance policies vary, and to a large extent they depend on the size of the class. In those huge lecture courses, your professor will have a ton of material to present during each session and probably won't spend precious minutes checking the roll. In smaller classes, however, a high premium is placed on individual student participation, and the professor will expect you to be on hand to carry your share of the discussion. So will your fellow students; if you're absent, their chances of being called on are increased.

As a group, colleges and universities seem far less rigid now about class attendance than they were a generation ago. Many professors, however, still impose harsh attendance policies for their classes, and they are confident of the full backing of their deans and presidents if those attendance policies are challenged.

Q What will the professor look for in grading my papers?

A First the professor will examine your work in and of itself, then go beyond that to seek out comparative differences between your work and that of someone else. Paper X is fairly strong; Paper Y is somewhat weaker; Paper Z is clearly the best of the lot. Paper Z gets an A, Paper X a B, and Paper Y a C. (This is all much easier said than done; profs may in fact spend hefty chunks of time arriving at those frail distinctions.)

But what do such phrases as "weaker" and "fairly strong" actually mean? They are judgment calls, arrived at in unique and highly personal ways. Some professors look upon grading as a positive thing. "Nice paragraph," you can almost hear them remark as they pore over an essay exam. "This was a key point . . . seemed to get the essence of the argument here . . . showed some understanding of this concept . . . fairly strong conclusion." Profs with this point of view tend to start the student out with zero, then award points for the admirable things they discover in the paper. Other teachers come at papers from the opposite end. They spot the student a full 100 points at the outset, then take away points for the faults they find. "This argument is only half made . . . unpersuasive reasoning . . . lousy punctuation . . . three misspelled words in one paragraph! . . . the entire second page rambles . . . careless sense of organization . . . fairly weak conclusion." In each case, the grade on the paper may come out the same; it's just that the graders got there by different routes.

Despite the differences in grading styles—and there are as many of these as there are professors—each teacher will most likely evaluate your work according to three broad criteria:

- Knowledge (your familiarity with the material).
- Judgment (to separate the important from the unimportant).

- Skill (your ability to present your arguments with clarity, polish, and conviction).

Beyond that, some teachers are favorably impressed or put off by some things more than others. A number of professors are notorious pushovers for good writing; it doesn't seem to matter much what you write, just as long as you write gracefully. Others are impressed when students use the technical terms that are a part of the vocabulary of the course; this suggests that they are immersing themselves in the subject matter. Still others place an unusually high premium on organization; students who carefully and emphatically outline their answers, listing and supporting key points one by one, invariably do well with these profs.

Shrewd students learn from what their professors say and write and then prepare and present their work accordingly. Important clues can be found early in the semester. The typical professor will assign a short paper or hour-long exam that seems important at the time but probably won't count for much in determining the final grade for the course. Carefully analyze the professor's comments on this paper. They will help you understand what the professor is looking for and can help you improve your test-taking and essay-writing skills.

 ## How are grades for the course determined?

This depends on the professor and the grading system employed. In some classes, the prof has developed specific objectives for you in the belief that your progress can be precisely measured. You'll find yourself evaluated not only in the context of the current semester but against the work of other students who have taken this course in the past. This is the kind of grading you're used to from high school, where there's a predetermined scale that covers all possible performance levels. (A grade of 90 to 100, for example, might be an A, 80 to 89 a B, and so on.) Your class average, your point on the scale, determines your grade for the course. Under this absolute grading system, every member of the class could conceivably get an A in the course. Or nobody could get an A.

Other teachers regard each class as an entity unto itself, and grades are decided by how each student performs in relation to the other students in that class. Using this approach, the top students would get A's, even if their averages were, say, 89, which would be a B under the other system. After the top grades are determined, the professor then curves the grades downward: If the students in the first group get an A, then those in the runner-up group, not quite as good, should get a B, and so on. In theory at least, professors using the curve system would award an equal number of F's and A's, and an equal number of B's and D's, and the largest group, the bell of the curve, would get C's. This rarely happens, by the way, because classes don't normally fall into such convenient patterns.

Professors who curve their grades—and many do, at least to some extent—begin with a number of basic assumptions about each class, among them: (1) most students are average, so the largest percentage of grades should be in the C range; (2) in each class at least one student should make an A; and (3) somebody should flunk. These are chancy propositions, and only the most literal-minded profs refuse to abandon or modify them during the semester as circumstances dictate. Students often resent the curve system, because it places them in head-to-head competition with their classmates. And it *is* demoralizing, that first day of class, when a truly first-class student walks into the room. You can almost hear the groans: "There goes the curve!"

In recent years there's been a sharp increase in the percentage of good grades awarded. "Grade inflation" or "grade-flation," it's often called. And, indeed, for many professors and students the average grade now appears to be not a C but a B, and any student who does slightly above average work may feel entitled to an A. Some academicians think this upward trend began during the Vietnam war; many professors were reluctant to give anything but top grades because they knew any male student who flunked out of college faced an odds-on chance of being drafted and sent into combat. Other observers trace the grade-flation phenomenon to the advent of student evaluations of teaching; fearful of low evaluations, professors began freely awarding high grades to keep their students happy. For whatever the reason, there are a lot of cheap A's and B's floating around out there.

You'll find that some grades mean more to you than others. You'll be prouder of that B awarded to you by a tough prof in a difficult course than of an easy B you picked up someplace else. The trouble is, both count the same on the transcript and in computing the GPA. One wishes the grading system—flawed as it is already—could at least be a little more consistent.

Q How can I score points with my professors?

 First, come to class. Second, appear interested in what the professor is saying. Third, ask intelligent questions. In other words, involve yourself in the course, and the brownie points will take care of themselves.

Professors appreciate enthusiastic students, and consciously or subconsciously they find ways to show their appreciation when grades are handed out. This doesn't mean you can blatantly suck up to a teacher and be rewarded with an A for your trouble. I am suggesting, however, that professors are human, and that they tend to treat people as they themselves wish to be treated.

It's difficult, perhaps, for students to understand how much the success of a class depends on the attitudes of the students themselves, quite apart from anything professors do or don't do. A teacher may love her 10 o'clock class and, as a result, become inspired to do a superlative job with it. At the same time, she may dislike or even dread the class she has at 11; these students are unprepared, dull, bored—and therefore boring. Each class has a distinct personality. If you can help set a positive tone for your class, through your genuine enthusiasm and active participation, you'll get better instruction and almost certainly a better grade.

On the other hand, if you cut class often, yawn visibly and/or audibly when you are there, doze off, read the student newspaper, or do your nails while the professor is trying to teach, you'll help make the class a dreary one for all concerned. You'll also probably get a poor grade, which you will deserve. A few teachers are able to psych themselves up for each class meeting and deliver a top professional performance regardless of the circumstances. Most professors, however, need positive feedback from students to bring out their best teaching efforts. Performers—and teachers, alas, are performers—need a *live* audience.

Good questions help also, and don't be bashful about asking them. Use some judgment, however, and don't repeatedly ask questions that call attention to yourself or belabor the obvious to your professor and your fellow students. The best questions are those that lead to a wider understanding of the material, clarify important issues, and nail down loose ends.

The number and caliber of questions can serve as a barometer to the success of the lecture. Over the years I've invited a number of guest speakers to talk to my students; afterwards I ask the visitors how they felt their talk had gone. "I'm pretty pleased with it," is a typical response. "Lots of bright questions. Who was that kid in the front row, the one who asked me about Watergate? Bright guy. Good student, I imagine." If he wasn't before, he is now.

Q What's the difference between an Assistant Professor and an Associate Professor?

A On a few campuses the teachers are unranked, as in high schools, but for the most part, college and university faculty members are assigned ranks that reflect their length of service and, presumably, their scholarly and professional achievement. The faculty members on the lowest rungs of the academic ladder are called Instructors or Lecturers. The next step, one at which new Ph.D.'s often begin, is that of Assistant Professor. After several years—four to seven, typically—Assistant Professors who have done well (or have somehow convinced colleagues and deans they've done well) may be promoted to the rank of Associate Professor. Eventually some of these Associates will be promoted to "full professor" or, as it's officially called, Professor.

Some institutions honor their most distinguished faculty members with "super ranks," which signify an endowed position and a higher salary. If you see someone listed as "University Professor of Economics," for example, or "Truman Langdon Professor of Chemistry," you can assume the individual has brought the institution special prestige and is being rewarded for it.

At the other end of the scale are the part-time faculty, called AIs (Assistant Instructors) or, more commonly, TAs (Teaching Assistants). For the most part, these are advanced graduate students who are getting classroom teaching experience and financial support while they're working on their doctorates. Many undergraduate classes, especially at the freshman level, are taught by TAs, and if you attend a large university you'll almost certainly encounter several of them during your first year or two. This is not necessarily bad; TAs are often effective and caring teachers, and many undergraduates actually prefer them to some of the full-time faculty, who are older and perhaps more remote.

 What should I call my professor?

A "Professor" is the proper form of address at all levels. (Don't call her "Associate Professor Jones," even if that is her actual rank.) You're also safe in referring to Mr. Smith, your history teacher, as "Doctor Smith," even if you're not sure whether he has his Ph.D. You'll rarely be corrected, even if you're wrong, for conferring a doctorate. TAs frequently prefer to be addressed by their first names, and if so, they'll tell you. Otherwise, call them "Mr." or "Ms." as the case may be.

Q What is tenure? Why—and how—is it awarded?

A Tenure is permanence of position, and a professor who's been granted tenure normally can't be fired unless (1) flagrant personal or professional misconduct is proved, or (2) the institution itself falls into financial jeopardy. In normal circumstances, then, tenure means a lifetime of job security.

Why do colleges confer tenure? That's a fair question, one frequently posed by hard-working businessmen who must continue to justify their own positions year after year in a highly competitive environment. To them, academic tenure seems certain to stifle ambition and condone mediocrity. (A few university presidents, acutely aware of some expensive but unproductive faculty members, might privately agree.) Essentially, however, tenure is designed to protect professors from political pressure. A college or university is supposed to serve as an open forum for ideas, many of which might be unpopular, radical, or even hateful to some citizens. Not everybody understands this. "Are your political science professors still teaching communism?" an angry congressman once demanded of a university president. "Yes, I suppose we are," the president replied. "Just as I guess we're still teaching cancer in the medical school."

Tenure represents the most profound and costly commitment an institution can make to a teacher. Because of this, it is not lightly conferred. The professor must first serve a period of probation, sometimes as long as six or seven years, during which time he or she can readily be dismissed. At the end of the probation period, most campuses force a decision—up or out. They either promote the individual and award tenure or give notice.

During the time the professor is being considered for tenure, many persons are consulted: faculty colleagues, the department chair, the academic dean, current students, former students, individuals from other campuses. The criteria for tenure vary from one school to the next, but normally they relate to the individual's teaching, research and publications, and service to the profession or institution. Research counts for a great deal at many colleges, while teaching ability is the primary consideration at others. Often special committees are convened to examine each tenure case. An individual tenure review usually takes several months to complete.

Once tenure is granted (normally the board of trustees, acting on the president's recommendation, will make the final decision), the professor is free to do his or her best work without fear of undue external (or internal) interference. This is a marvelous privilege. Some faculty members abuse it. Most don't.

Q Why is it that professors must "publish or perish"? Isn't teaching more important than research?

A At some colleges and universities, young professors are awarded raises, promotions, and tenure on the basis of their ability to teach. Period. On other campuses, however, the professors are expected to create new knowledge as well. They attempt to discover new findings that can widen the scope of the field, or they reinterpret old knowledge in innovative and improved ways. Good teaching, to a large extent, is assumed (often mistakenly).

New research is written up and offered to scholarly journals, of which there are a great many in all areas, or to the publishers of scholarly books. The best research studies, as determined by experts who serve as juries or referees, are published in these journals, often called *refereed* journals. When a professor has an article accepted for publication, it means that his or her research has been carefully studied and is now recommended as a genuine contribution to the scholarship of the field.

On the other hand, rejection of the professor's research (many more manuscripts are turned down than are published) is generally interpreted to mean that he or she isn't saying anything new or worthwhile and thus not really contributing to knowledge and not developing as a scholar. On some highly competitive, research-oriented campuses, a young faculty member may need to have published up to six or more articles or books to qualify for promotion and tenure. Fewer publications than this and the administration might well decide to dismiss this individual and seek a replacement who might be more productive. Young professors, in other words, frequently feel great pressure to publish or perish.

The situation can be absurd, of course, and every university has its share of horror stories about splendid teachers who were fired because they didn't publish, while other teachers who behaved like babbling fools in the classroom were promoted and tenured because they had managed to publish meaningless research in obscure, and largely unread, scholarly journals. Some universities have their priorities for faculty all wrong, and it's often the students who get shortchanged in the process.

Ideally, of course, teaching and research go together. Some of the most brilliant teachers are those who are also deeply immersed in research, men and women who themselves continue to study and learn, and share their excitement with their students. But there are other fine teachers, too, who work well with students and love being in the classroom but are simply not interested in doing research. These faculty members, the best of them, anyway, are not lazy or inept; they just happen to prefer teaching to scholarship. The system ought to be able to reward these individuals too, but in a great many tragic cases it doesn't.

So if that likeable young professor in your Economics 260 class sometimes seems preoccupied, it may be because his mind at that moment is on his research or, in a larger sense, on his survival.

CHAPTER 4

AFTER HOURS

How much time, each week you're in college, do you think you'll spend *outside* the classroom? Try 90 percent. There are 168 hours in a week, and assuming a normal class load and no absences, your in-class time will average only about 16 hours—rarely more than 20. Figure in the time you can reasonably expect to spend eating, sleeping, commuting, studying, even holding down a part-time job, and you're still left with more than a few hours to manage, or mismanage, on your own.

Ideally you'll devote some of this time to keeping yourself in shape, working toward the goal of *mens sana in corpore sano*—a sound mind in a sound body. But there are other dimensions to consider as well, such as those involving personality. Your ability to function in social situations isn't the kind of thing that's taught in the classroom. Or if it is, it's not taught very extensively or very well. You learn this best on your own—by getting to know lots of people from different backgrounds and by exposing yourself to new viewpoints and ways of thinking different from any you've heard before. After hours.

 # How do I meet people?

There are all sorts of ways to meet people on a college campus. Because the atmosphere is usually open and friendly (except during exam week, when you shouldn't be socializing anyway), introducing yourself should become an easy, natural thing to do.

At the beginning of the semester, college is an endless line, and you'll spend hours waiting with other students to pay your fees, get your health card, have your I.D. mug shot taken, write a check for your textbooks, pick up class cards at registration and on drop/add/change day, and so on. You continue standing in line throughout the academic year—three times a day in the cafeteria, to check out books at the library, to get tickets to ball games and concerts. The point is that these lines offer a natural opportunity for you to start talking to the person behind you, even if he or she isn't your "type," whatever that means. You can never be sure. If you are normally shy, force yourself to become friendlier. What can you lose? Maybe the person you speak to is just as shy, just as interesting, and has been waiting for someone else to go first.

And this seems as good a place as any to offer this suggestion: Don't look at every member of the opposite sex as a potential girlfriend or boyfriend or think of every person you date as your future mate for life. Just enjoy contact with that individual for what it is, without expecting that it necessarily must lead somewhere. A student couple can become friends without ever becoming romantically involved, and these friendships can be most rewarding. Getting bogged down too soon in a romance can be devastating for a freshman, especially if it leads to isolation from everyone else. Even worse, there are some students who won't get to know, much less go on a date with, another student who is not a jock or a preppy or whatever it is he or she is determined to be or find in a spouse. It's entirely possible and often highly desirable to have a cup of coffee or a Coke or see a movie with someone without worrying about what future the relationship may have.

But don't just stand in line. Get busy. Join the French Club or the campus newspaper or yearbook staff, try out for a part in a dramatic production, volunteer for work in student government—whatever it takes to involve yourself with people whose interests are similar to your own. Ask to borrow someone's notes from biology class and, when you return them, offer to buy coffee or lunch to show your gratitude.

Other good places to meet people include sorority or fraternity houses, health spas or running tracks, or plays or concerts.

And of course there are local houses of worship. Many provide free or very inexpensive suppers for college students. Congregations also arrange picnics, skating and bowling parties, and other events for the college crowd. There are lots of possibilities here. And think how pleased and relieved your mom would be if you phoned to say, "I'm going to the Homecoming game with this nice woman I met at church. . . . Yes, that's right, mother, at church."

Q Is it all right to share expenses on a date?

A Sure, unless one or both of you would feel your principles were being compromised. If the woman is willing to go Dutch, the man might find it wise as well as gracious to accept once in a while. It almost certainly beats spending a lonely Saturday night in your dorm while she's doing the same in hers. On some campuses, going Dutch is the norm. Pooling your resources makes sense, especially in these difficult times. Another possibility is to take turns; you pay all the expenses for one date, she funds the next one. Just try to work out the details in advance.

Again, this assumes that both of you find this acceptable. If either of you doesn't, then don't push. It's far better to date less often or less extravagantly than to have a falling-out over who picks up the check.

Incidentally, you'll find the college campus a surprisingly informal and unpretentious place, despite the ritzy image many outsiders have of it. Most college students are broke at some point; for others, poverty is a more or less continuous condition. But if all dating waited until students had ample funds with which to entertain in first-class style, there would be far less socializing than there is.

Beyond that, much social activity on campus these days seems to be not couples "dating," as such, but entire groups of men and women going places together, sharing and sharing alike on expenses.

Q Any ideas for cheap entertainment?

A Because so many students share the same condition, namely destitution, you should feel no embarrassment whatsoever about being unable to entertain your date in the grand manner (he or she is probably not accustomed to it, anyway). Don't be so concerned about bedazzling your dates; charming them is less important than simply communicating with them. In other words, you should try to express, not merely impress.

With a little imagination, even the most severely limited budgets can create some memorable social engagements. At Gordon College in Wenham, Massachusetts, resourceful students, in the hallowed tradition of impoverished scholars everywhere, compiled a list of fifty suggestions for dates that cost less than $5 each. Here are some of their ideas:

Cheer on the basketball team . . . attend a free concert or recital . . . make a late-night coffee date or a breakfast date to start the morning . . . take a scenic drive . . . support your local campus artists by attending a showing . . . share a pizza . . . get tickets for a campus play, movie, or variety show . . . invite someone over for Monopoly and popcorn . . . see a movie in the afternoon before the prices go up . . . spend nineteen quarters on video games . . . play Scrabble and sip hot chocolate on those cold nights . . . browse around a local shopping center or mall . . . play Ping-Pong in the dormitory . . . take a study break at a nearby snack shop . . . play tennis . . . play Ultimate Frisbee on the quad . . . fly a kite in the park . . . have a picnic at a quiet spot . . . play miniature golf . . . skate on the ice rink . . . hike through a nearby forest . . . stage a snowball fight . . . try canoeing or rock-climbing or spend a day at the beach of a nearby state park.

Q My girlfriend and I have gone steady throughout high school. We'll be in college together, and we want to get married. What are the chances for success of a student marriage?

A When this question is posed to me, as it has been a number of times, I hastily refer it to the counseling office, and even there, among the trained psychologists, there is an obvious reluctance to comment in general terms about so important and personal a topic.

After warning that each case is unique, however, here's how one college counselor replied: "I frankly tell students that the odds are against a successful marriage in this situation. The problems with any marriage—problems with money, sex, in-laws—seem to be intensified in a college marriage. There's also the matter of getting used to each other, insisting that one spouse behave the way the other spouse wants him or her to. The behavior patterns of college students are obviously different in many ways from those of high school students.

"The young marrieds work all day, then come home at night—with hours of studying they know they ought to do—and they are exhausted. Some men thought they were impotent, but after a vacation they found they were not. They had just been working too hard. The old story of getting your degree and your divorce at the same time is too often true here."

Another counselor at a different campus put it this way: "The first years of our lives are spent in what might be called the 'dependent' stage. Next comes the 'independent' period, a time for spreading wings, for exploring, for thinking and acting on one's own. Marriage represents still another stage, that of 'interdependence.' Until now, any young person has probably thought of the world in terms of 'me.' But after marriage, it's supposed to become 'we.' 'We' is the operational unit for planning, for socializing, for earning and spending money, for everything. Many students aren't ready to begin thinking as 'we' just yet, which suggests they may not be mature enough to sustain a marriage relationship."

Now, having reported all that, let me interject that my wife and I were married as students more than twenty-five years ago. In our case, we found that the difficulties—the hard work, the grinding poverty—actually brought us closer together. But other student couples, friends of ours, weren't so lucky; their marriages didn't survive. It is of course possible that they wouldn't have anyway—that is, that the college environment wasn't a factor one way or the other.

It would seem terribly important, then, to know where you and your spouse-to-be are situated on the dependent/independent/interdependent scale before you contemplate a college marriage—or a marriage of any kind, for that matter.

Q Is the threat of rape on college campuses real or exaggerated? What can I do for protection?

A Here are two grim statistics: One out of every 4 American women, according to FBI projections, will be the victim of rape or sexual assault at least once in her lifetime. One out of every 24 American women will become the object of an attempted rape this year.

Rape is the fastest-growing crime of violence in the country. In the years from 1977 to 1986, the number of rapes increased by 42 percent. Worse yet, rape is a crime most colleges and universities clearly are not geared to combat. The typical campus police force is at minimal strength, especially in these austere budgetary times. The campuses are not well lighted; those beautifully secluded spots, landscaped in a far more innocent era, provide ideal cover for a would-be attacker.

Students who rent apartments near the campus find themselves living in neighborhoods populated by transients. Strangers aren't noticed as they would be in older, more settled parts of town.

For all these reasons, it's important that women exercise extreme caution. Here are some of the preventive measures suggested by campus and community women's groups:

WHEN YOU WALK
- Walk with friends whenever possible.
- Don't walk in areas where you aren't sure it's safe.
- Walk with a purpose. Look confident even if you aren't.
- If assistance is available, use it. As a matter of policy, many schools have security guards who will, if requested, walk women to their homes late at night.
- Don't hitchhike. Ever.

IN YOUR CAR
- Keep your car in good working order and always have at least a quarter of a tank of gas.
- Always keep car doors locked—when driving or parked.
- Have your keys ready as you approach your car.
- Park in areas that are well lighted.
- Check the back seat before you get in.

JOGGING
- Try to find a partner; avoid jogging alone.
- Vary your route.
- Jog in populated areas.
- Get to know some of the people in the neighborhood in case of an emergency.

IN SOCIAL SITUATIONS
- It will increase your safety if you let your roommate, friends, or parents know where you are going, whom you'll be with, and when you expect to be home.
- If you take drugs or drink, it will be more difficult for you to exercise good judgment, particularly in unfamiliar situations. If a date is drinking excessively or taking drugs, get out of the situation as quickly as possible and find another way home.
- Develop a support system with friends. If you see a young woman being pushed or talked into something she doesn't want, offer your help (a ride home, talk to the young man, etc.).

But protecting yourself from strangers is just a part of the problem.

Q How prevalent is "date rape" on campus?

A Many rapes—most, by some estimates—are committed not by ski-masked hoodlums who attack strangers on dark streets, but rather by individuals whom the victim knows well enough to go out with socially. "Date rape" is a matter of growing concern on college campuses, as it is throughout society. Increasing numbers of college women have been forced by acquaintances and dates to submit to sexual intercourse against their will.

Indeed, a recent study of 6,500 students, financed by the National Institute on Mental Health and conducted by Professor Mary Koss of Kent State University, revealed that more than 10 percent of the coeds questioned—actually, about 1 out of 8—had been forced to have sex without their consent. In this survey, 9 out of every 10 students who had been raped *knew their assailants.* Nearly half of these sexual assaults, 47 percent, were committed by first dates or romantic acquaintances.

And while a number of men who were interviewed admitted having forcible sex with unwilling partners, none was willing to identify himself as a rapist.

Indeed, much date rape seems to result from misread signals—a woman's "no" being interpreted as a come on. "Some men have the capacity to fool themselves into thinking that date rape is normal behavior," said one clinical psychologist at Ohio State in an interview with the *New York Times*. "They believe the myth that when a woman says no, she really means yes."

This and other misbegotten notions are being dealt with in conferences held on campuses around the country. In one of these, held at the University of Wisconsin and sponsored by a group called Men Stopping Rape, women and men acted out anxieties and frustrations they typically experienced on dates. Failure in communication emerged as a major triggering cause of date rape. Ironically, during these date rape discussions a number of women felt they themselves were to blame—for overlooking some character flaw in their dates or using poor judgment—and wondered what they had said or done to provoke the assault.

Perhaps because of this clearly misplaced sense of guilt, the overwhelming majority of date rape victims compound their problem by not talking about it to friends and counselors who could offer support. Nine out of ten cases of date rape are never reported to the police.

Q Are there danger signals to indicate the possibility of date rape?

A Yes, according to the National Organization for Victim Assistance, and here are some of them:

- Be wary when your relationship seems to be operating along classic stereotypes of dominant male and submissive female. Some men, particularly in late adolescence, are very domineering, putting the woman in a poor position to assert himself. If a man orders for you in a restaurant, plans all date activities, and always gets his way, chances are that he will do the same thing in an intimate setting.
- Be wary when a date tries to control your behavior in any way—for example, trying to restrict the people you meet or forcing you to do something you don't want to do. Be especially wary of men who pressure you, knowing that you would be too embarrassed to tell mutual friends or that you would not be believed. All these things make you more vulnerable.
- Avoid giving ambiguous messages. For example, don't engage in petting, then say you don't want to go any further, then return to petting. If it is clear in your mind that you don't intend to have sex with someone

you are dating, be clear about it. Communicating your intentions openly can diffuse a possibly difficult situation.

- When dating someone for the first time, try to go with a group. This is especially important for young people.

Q What if I am sexually assaulted?

A Authorities recommend that you tell the police. Unfortunately, only a small percentage of sexual assaults ever get reported. Many rapists commit the crime repeatedly. Your notifying the police might help someone else.

Also, you should get medical treatment right away at any emergency room, from your personal physician, or at a health clinic. You may be injured internally, or you may have been exposed to AIDS or venereal disease; there is also the possibility of pregnancy.

Two don'ts: (1) Don't immediately bathe or shower, and (2) don't destroy the clothes you were wearing at the time, tempted as you may be to do so. Valuable evidence could be lost.

As soon as you are able to, write down a complete description of the assailant and as many details of the crime as you can recall.

Reporting a rape and pressing charges, I know, are far easier said by me than done by you. Indeed, most rape victims, understandably, seem to want to forget their trauma, not compound it with the added stress brought on by the police, publicity, and the courts. There have been horror stories about police skepticism, about the social and emotional pressure placed on the victim, about the difficulty prosecutors have in obtaining a conviction in rape cases. But attitudes and sensitivities are changing for the better. Police and prosecutors are far more sympathetic, and certainly they take rape far more seriously than they did even a few years ago. Much of this heightened consciousness is due to the courageous women who did recognize sexual violence for the profoundly serious crime that it is—and were willing to fight back.

Q What do I do if I get an obscene or crank phone call?

A The Division of Law Enforcement and Safety at the University of South Carolina suggests the following:

- Hang up as soon as you hear an obscenity, an improper question, or no response to your hello.
- Don't play detective. Don't prolong the call by trying to figure out who is calling.
- Remain calm. Or, if you do get upset or angry or frightened, don't let the caller know it.
- Don't attempt to be clever. A witty response might be taken as a sign of encouragement.
- Don't attempt counseling. The obscene caller obviously does need professional help but will only be encouraged by your concern and may continue the calls.
- Don't tell everyone you know about your calls. Many calls of this type are actually made by "friends."
- Report obscene or annoying calls to your campus police department.

Moreover, it's a good idea to avoid volunteering your phone number to an unknown caller. This is an invitation to call again. If your number was called by mistake, the caller doesn't need to know your number.

Too, it's a good idea to be cautious if and when you place a classified ad. Use a newspaper box or post office box number if possible. If you must use your phone number, don't list your address. Crank callers, police report, are avid readers of the classified ads.

Q **My parents are worried about drugs on campus. How bad is the drug problem?**

A Not as bad in some respects, many observers think, as it was fifteen years ago. During the mid-seventies, increasing numbers of students began turning away from hard drugs and back to alcohol. This caused some momentary rejoicing, of course, until the realization slowly sank in that alcohol itself is a drug, perhaps the most insidious one available.

Experts in the field, including counselors, physicians, residence hall directors, and people on the staff of the dean of students at several institutions, all report a considerable decline in the use of *some* hard drugs on their campuses. Some of the pills (amphetamines, barbiturates, etc.) are harder to get now, and more young people seem to have become aware of the truly frightening consequences of heroin, angel dust, and the like. The illegal use of these drugs has dropped by 50 percent since 1980, experts believe.

Cocaine is a different story. Dr. Lloyd D. Johnson, a director of a massive study, "Drug Use Among American High School Students, College Students, and Other Young Adults: National Trends Through 1985," reported that 17 percent of all college students used cocaine within the past year, and about 30 percent of all college students will have tried the drug at least once by the end of their senior year. "The most serious current problem clearly is the fact that cocaine use remains at peak levels in this population," he wrote. "This is also true of high school students and young adults generally, not just college students."

Dr. Johnson, of the Institute for Social Research at the University of Michigan, added that "students report cocaine to be fairly readily available and, until very recently, at least, the great majority saw little risk in experimenting with it"—this despite the harsh publicity the drug has received. The study, financed by the National Institute on Drug Abuse, concluded that "clearly this nation's high school students and other young adults still show a level of involvement with illicit drugs which is greater than can be found in any other industrialized nation in the world."

A cheap, powerful derivative of cocaine, crack has affected thousands of lives since it first appeared in the United States in the early 1980s. It is already regarded as the nation's most serious, and most frightening, drug problem. And though crack's influence is most tragically observed among inner-city ghetto children and teenagers, the highly addictive drug has, to at least some degree, invaded the university community as well.

Marijuana is present on most campuses, readily available on many, and used in great quantities on others. Student use of marijuana, however, appears to be declining; 51 percent of college students were pot smokers in 1980; by 1985 the figure was estimated at 42 percent. "There's no pattern here," one campus housing director said. "Marijuana consumption cuts across racial and social lines. A few years ago you could work up a profile of a typical marijuana user. Not anymore. I'm continually astonished at the number and type of students we find smoking pot." Most students accept marijuana as a fact of college life, and pot smokers aren't ostracized as they were many years ago.

This benevolent tolerance does not extend to the campus administrators, however, who still must comply with the laws that prohibit the use of controlled substances. Quite a few officials will look the other way when it comes to marijuana, but many do not. If you are caught, you probably won't be expelled—not for a first offense, anyway—but repeated violations could get you kicked out of your dorm (for breaching the housing contract you signed), and you may find the sudden change of address awkward to explain back home. Drug *dealing,* of course, is a far more serious offense, one that is almost certain to get you expelled from school and prosecuted by civil authorities.

In general terms, though, you'll probably find the college drug scene no worse—and in some cases actually less serious—than the one you faced in high school. And, given the additional maturity you've presumably acquired by now, you should be able to handle peer pressure more confidently.

Most students, in fact, seem less vulnerable to the temptation of cocaine and marijuana than they are to alcohol abuse. "Eighty percent of the student problems I deal with," grumbled one experienced housing director, "are connected directly to booze. I'm talking about disorderly conduct, damage in the residence halls, arrest reports, personal troubles, flunk-outs—these are primarily alcohol-related. The biggest offenders are freshman men—kids who try to knock off three fifths of bourbon in a weekend. It's a macho thing with them, I guess, though many became seasoned drinkers before they ever left high school."

An associate dean of students has this to say: "I'm amazed at the number of students who begin drinking even before noon. Instead of a cup of coffee, they get a beer. Many seem unable to function—much less have fun—without alcohol. The party revolves around the bar or the keg. For too many of these kids, alcohol is the crutch."

Q Do I HAVE to drink in college?

A No, of course not. Not any more than you have to eat spinach or cauliflower if you don't want to. In all likelihood, no one is going to force a drink on you or make a big deal out of it if you say, "No, thanks," when booze is served. There will probably be less pressure, in fact, than you found in high school.

What can you do? If you're really uncomfortable, you can make up an excuse or nurse one drink all evening without guzzling it. Or you can just tell the truth; you'd rather not drink. What's the worst thing that can happen to you? Nothing. A look or a comment, maybe, and after that you're home free. In fact, you'll find that plenty of people will admire your values and your self-control.

If you really are worried, however, there are other alternatives:

- Stay away from parties where the primary objective is to get smashed. The folks who attend these blasts won't remember the next day whether you were there or not anyway.

- Join a support group. There are a number of these already in existence and others are being formed. Your college may well have a chapter of Bacchus or SADD (Students Against Drunk Driving) or a similar organization. There are students everywhere who are concerned about alcohol abuse; it shouldn't be difficult to get in touch with them.
- Some larger campuses have dorms or houses that are, by the choice of the students who live in them, reserved for nondrinkers. You can check into this possibility at your school.
- You might be more comfortable at a church-related or other college or university where drinking is an official no-no. At these institutions abstinence is easy; since you'd be risking suspension to drink, you have a perfect excuse to stay sober. Church schools, by the way, are not populated exclusively by sissies; if you don't believe me, ask anyone who's ever played football against the Baylor Bears.

These are all serious, and probably unnecessary, steps for most of you, though. There's really no need to rearrange your life just to dodge the problem of alcohol. Whatever else college life is, it's manifestly a place that cherishes the principle of *laissez-faire;* in other words, what you do—or don't do—is largely your own business, unless it gets out of control.

Q. How can I tell if I (or a friend) may be developing an alcohol problem?

A It's important to realize that anyone, regardless of age, sex, education, or social status, can become a victim of alcohol abuse. College students, as any halfway observant professor can tell you, emphatically are not immune.

If you or a roommate or a friend is wondering if your drinking has passed the socializing stage, then ask yourself the following questions (they are adapted from the short version of the Michigan Alcoholism Screening Test). Each time you answer "yes," place a checkmark on a piece of paper.

1. Do you drink more than most other people?
2. Does your roommate or friend ever worry or complain about your drinking?
3. Do you ever feel guilty about your drinking?
4. Do friends or relatives think you drink more than most people?
5. Do you ever experience a loss of control? (That is, you fully meant to drink only one or two drinks, but end up having more than you intended?)

6. Have you ever attended a meeting of Alcoholics Anonymous because of your drinking?
7. Has drinking ever created problems between you and your roommate or between you and a parent or other near relative?
8. Have you ever gotten in trouble at work (or in class) because of your drinking?
9. Have you ever neglected your obligations, your family, or your classes for two or more days in a row because you were drinking?
10. Have you ever gone to anyone for help about your drinking?
11. Have you ever been in a hospital because of drinking?
12. Have you ever been arrested for drunken driving, driving while intoxicated, or driving under the influence of alcoholic beverages?
13. Have you ever been arrested, even for a few hours, because of other drunken behavior?

If you have only one checkmark on your paper, it's not likely that you have a problem. Two checkmarks mean you might have a problem. Three or more mean there is a good possibility you do have a problem and should seek counseling.

If you're still uncertain about your drinking, try one more test. Set a limit for yourself. One expert suggestion is that you make sure you don't drink every day, and that you drink no more than three drinks on the days when you do drink. (A drink here is defined as one twelve-ounce can or bottle of beer, a four-ounce glass of wine, or a mixed drink with one ounce of 86-proof distilled spirits.) If you discover that you're unable to keep to this limit, you may need help.

 ## What is Rush Week?

Rush Week is the time when people in Greek letter fraternities and sororities seek out, or "rush," the new students in hopes of recruiting a good crop of pledges to sustain their organizations. It's a mutual selection process, with the new students, or rushees, hoping to choose the ideal Greek organizations for them. Each fraternity and sorority is limited by rush rules to issuing a certain number of invitations to join (these are called bids); each rushee can accept only one bid, so the mutual selection process sometimes misfires. Rush, in other words, can get pretty brutal, and many students choose to forego Rush Week and Greek life altogether. Others, conversely, find Rush Week exhilarating, a delicious whirlwind of parties filled with new faces and new friends.

While the ritual is conducted differently on each campus, and the fraternity rush is usually far less tightly structured than the sorority rush, the ultimate goal—matching the rushee's top choice with the fraternity or sorority's top choice—remains the same. Here's how the sorority rush works at one midwestern campus:

On a Sunday late in August, a week or so before classes begin, the registrants for rush assemble on the campus for an orientation meeting with representatives of the Panhellenic Council, the outfit that regulates rush procedures. The rushees then move into dormitory rooms where they'll sleep, or try to sleep, between the strenuous rounds of parties that follow during the next days and nights. Some kind of general entertainment or informal social program may be scheduled for all the rushees later that evening.

The next two days are devoted to open-house parties, short receptions of thirty minutes or so designed to bring every rushee into every sorority house on the campus. From these brief encounters, the rushees are supposed to begin narrowing their choices a bit for the next round of parties, the invitationals.

The invitational parties are longer and somewhat more elaborate, and the objective here is to provide smaller groups of rushees with a better impression of the personalities of the individual sororities. Each rushee can sign up for as many as ten invitationals. The sororities, meanwhile, have done some narrowing down of their own; they may choose to extend a smaller number of invitations in order to concentrate on the rushees they consider especially promising.

After the invitationals come the final parties, the preferentials, or return parties. By this time each rushee is supposed to have narrowed her choices down to three. The sororities, too, knowing they have only a limited number of bids available, usually invite back only those rushees they regard as top prospects. These "pref" parties are usually more serious affairs, for most of the screening has been done by now.

When the preferential parties are over, the rushees retreat to their rooms to draw up a list of their sorority choices in order of preference. The sororities, usually after an all-night meeting, decide to whom they want to extend bids. Both the rushee preferences and the sorority bids are secret. A computer discreetly and dispassionately matches up the two. If a rushee listed Sorority A first and Sorority B second, but only received a bid from Sorority B, she will then receive a bid from Sorority B, and only she—not the sorority—will know that she didn't receive her top choice.

If you and your friends do go through Rush, let me offer two bits of advice. First, don't "suicide." A "suicide" is an all-or-nothing decision: "If I can't get into Sorority A, then I'm not interested in anything else." Give every group a good chance to get to know you, and keep an open mind throughout. Second, and more important, try not to take Rush Week too seriously. No matter how it comes out, you'll have the rest of your college years ahead of you.

What you are, and what you become, will be a great deal more important than anything that happens during Rush.

Q. How do I know if a fraternity or sorority is really for me?

A. The Greek system promotes fellowship—indeed, virtually compels it. Beginning with Rush Week (see p. 95), you and your fraternity brothers or sorority sisters will go through much together—everything from house cleanup to beer blasts to silly costume parties to fancy dress formals. This is the stuff of which friendships and memories are made. Some of the memories may be painful, and a few of the friendships may be more trouble than they are worth, but you have them anyway and in all probability will get downright misty-eyed as you recall them years from now.

There is something to be said for living among your friends, especially on a big, impersonal campus. At least within the fraternity or sorority house you feel you belong, that you aren't just floating along in limbo as one of thousands of faceless, numbered students that are processed and computerized into oblivion by the university.

And despite the Animal House image—which has some truth in it—fraternities and sororities *can* teach you something about social graces. This sounds less important than it actually is. The ability to meet and talk with people comfortably, to demonstrate polish and consideration in your dealings with others—these traits are much more appreciated than may be generally realized.

Greek life exacts its toll, however, and the price may be more than you care to pay. The relentless social whirl brings on what some students feel is a pressure to perform—to show up with a stunning date for every occasion, to think and act and dress in ways that will suitably impress all concerned. You may not sense this pressure and you really shouldn't, but many students do, and they often handle it poorly. The obligatory, hard-charging participation in *everything*—intramurals, service projects, parties, and dances—will drain away time and energy from your studies. Greek life also costs money. Dues, special assessments, pledge and initiation fees, gifts, party favors, photographs, and other miscellaneous items total several hundred dollars a year on the average. The potentially most damaging aspect of all is the danger Greek societies pose of perpetuating a questionable set of values. Greek life too often seems to place a premium on conformity and gloss. It starts with Rush Week and, for some, never ends.

So should you pledge? Only you can determine that for yourself. (Beware of anyone who wants to make the decision for you.) There is a certain snobbishness among some Greeks, no doubt, but there's also a reverse snob appeal, an anti-Greek sentiment that can be equally vicious and unfair. If you feel comfortable with a particular group and think you would enjoy the activities and the fellowship, then join. If you feel uneasy about the whole thing, then don't join. Neither decision is irreversible. You can consider pledging—or depledging—later.

While you're deliberating, however, you might take into account these two caveats:

- Don't pledge until you feel you really know something about the group and can place it in perspective. This means doing some homework; it may even require a delay in your going through Rush until you've lived on campus a while and seen all the Greeks in action. Rush Week, with all its giddy intensity, can be a miserably poor time to make a rational decision.
- Don't pledge a certain sorority or fraternity just because your mom or dad once belonged and you feel pressured to continue the family tradition. Greek houses undergo massive personality changes from one year to the next, and there's no way the old lodge can be the same today as it was a generation ago. Every fraternity and sorority has its legacies, and a fair number of them are colossal misfits. Look over all the houses carefully. Then, if you do pledge the family fraternity or sorority, you'll be sure you did so for the right reasons.

Q Should I get involved in student government?

A The student body at your college will be organized, if that is the word for it, into an official-sounding agency that (1) has some legislative authority in certain areas affecting student life and (2) represents the students to the real policymakers of the institution, such as the president and the Board of Trustees.

In truth, your Student Senate probably won't have much real clout. (Cynical students have referred to it as a "Tinkertoy democracy.") Participating in student government is, however, a good way to get to know people and to find out just how your campus community operates. Any number of successful careers in politics have been launched by campaigns for student government positions.

Campuswide elections, sometimes spirited affairs, are normally held in the spring. There may be a special election in the fall to choose officers for the new freshman class. If you want to stake out your claim as an up-and-coming student leader, these freshman elections are a good place to start.

If you don't want to seek an elective office but you still want to get involved, you can work on student government committees. There are usually quite a few of these, for recreation, student life, entertainment, cultural attractions, publicity, etc., and they offer attractive opportunities for service and leadership. These committees have much to say about how student activity fees are spent, so you could find yourself in on decisions about special events, convocation speakers, bringing top-name entertainment to campus, and managing the student union. Members of these committees are usually appointed by the elected student leaders, so if you'd like to serve, simply drop by the student government office and volunteer.

Q What is an intramural sports program?

A Intramural sports are played with enthusiasm, if not ferocity, on virtually every college campus. You hear most about flag football, a game that offers enough action to satisfy even the most aggressive student athlete, but the intramural program goes far beyond the gridiron. Individual, dual, and team activities are arranged to suit a whole spectrum of recreational preferences. The competition is as spirited, or as genteel, as you care to make it.

At Vanderbilt University, a school that has one of the more extensive intramural programs, the schedule includes soccer, volleyball, basketball, flag football, golf, table tennis, tennis, handball, racquetball, cross-country, billiards, punt-pass-and-kick, free-throw shooting, wrestling, swimming, diving, track and field, softball, and bowling.

Intramurals provide excellent fellowship and healthy recreation. They're great for clearing out the cobwebs after a long afternoon in the library or the physics lab.

Another nice thing about intramurals is that anybody can play. And thousands do—more than 50 percent of the students on many campuses. You don't have to try out; you just sign up. For team sports, you'll probably participate with your living group (dorm floor, sorority, town club, etc.). For individual and dual sports, you can register through the intramural office.

If you're *really* serious, you might go out for a club sport, such as rugby or water polo or even skydiving. Or maybe you'll want to register for a recreational sport as part of your academic schedule; these usually include swimming, tennis, racquetball, scuba diving, ballroom dancing, and aerobics. There may be an additional fee for some of these, for equitation, Karate Shito Ryu, or sailing, for example, but the charge will be only a tiny portion of what you would pay at a private club.

 ## How can I get to know international students?

At larger schools, contact the International Students Office; at smaller colleges, you might ask the dean of students for the name of the international student adviser.

The school administration can serve the official needs of international students by providing information about housing, academic regulations, schedules, and so on, but it cannot do everything necessary to make these visitors feel entirely at home in this new and complex environment. Consequently, many international students, who have worked hard for years to earn the privilege of studying in this country, end up being lonely and miserable during their stay here. When my wife and I invited several international students over for Thanksgiving dinner, we found that two of them, one from Hong Kong and one from Taiwan, had been off the campus only twice in three months. One had been downtown only once, and downtown is five blocks from the campus. American teachers and students have not always been very good hosts to international students. Perhaps you will do better.

To become acquainted with international students, simply ask the adviser to let you know of upcoming events sponsored by the International Students Association. Most colleges have an organization of this kind, even if there are only a few international students, and involvement by Americans is welcomed. Many international student associations put on a number of memorable social events. At a recent international student dinner at a large university, for example, the menu included shish kebab from Thailand, Chinese fried wonton, Vietnamese fried rice, Palestinian stuffed squash, German salad, Korean sauteed chicken, curried vegetables from India, and some spectacularly delicious dishes from Africa. The entertainment included Irish singers, dancing groups from Indonesia and Eastern Europe, and classical Spanish guitar music.

International students enrich your campus in so many ways, and getting to know them helps you widen your own horizons. They are bright students, and, in fact, some of them will eventually hold positions of great importance when they return home. Who knows? That shy, possibly lonely international

78770

student you meet today may become some nation's prime minister in a few years.

Q What opportunities are there for student volunteer work?

A Donating time and talent to worthy causes is a grand tradition among college students. Each year tens of thousands of student volunteers work on their campuses, in their communities, and with religious and government programs that take them across the world.

One bright coed I know contributed her communication and fund-raising skills to a successful campaign to help the local chapter of the Urban League put a black-oriented radio station on the air. Another student cooks breakfast and washes dishes four mornings a week at the community kitchen, while another puts in a dozen evenings a month as a nurses' aide and volunteer counselor at a community-run spouse-abuse center. A graduate student of mine, an industrious, self-supporting young man with a thousand things to do, still finds time to be a Big Brother to a child from a broken home. Other student volunteers read to the blind, work with emotionally disturbed children, become teachers' aides at inner-city schools, repair run-down houses in poverty areas, and conduct recreation programs in nursing homes and centers for battered children. The list could go on and on.

Somewhere on your campus is an office that coordinates volunteer efforts. The program may be run by the student government, the placement center, or the dean of students. You can quickly find out which agencies need volunteer help. Experience, though helpful, is usually not necessary. All you truly need are the interest, the dedication, and the time to share.

Q How important is it to take part in campus activities? Wouldn't I be better off studying instead?

A College students are fervent joiners. From the moment you arrive on campus, people will attempt to recruit you for clubs and causes that cover the waterfront of professional, political, religious, and social concerns.

Many of the clubs, frankly, don't amount to much. They convene early in the fall to elect officers, then schedule an "urgent meeting" later on to have their picture taken for the yearbook, and that's about it. Other student groups do meet regularly, and at great length, and involve their members in projects that can best be described as busywork. That's the negative view. On the positive side, campus activities bring freshmen into the social life of the school; develop talents, skills, and interests; foster friendships; and get would-be grinds out of the library once in a while.

A few student organizations actually do some good. Campus environmental groups on one southern campus helped mobilize enough public opinion to block a plan to strip-mine beautiful forest land that had been donated to the university. Black student groups have successfully diminished racism at some schools. Student clubs opposing alcohol abuse have done much to raise the level of awareness to this urgent problem. And the most interesting speakers on the campus, frequently, are not the ones on the official lecture schedule, but those controversial figures invited by a campus club. Not every campus club, in other words, should be dismissed as a huge waste of time and money.

But pick your clubs carefully. Join only those in which you have a legitimate interest and to which you feel you can make a contribution. Think twice about joining merely because, as you will so often hear, "it'll look good on your résumé." What really looks good on your résumé is a sparkling grade point average, which is especially hard to attain if you spend half your time in club meetings.

CHAPTER 5

WHEN YOU NEED HELP

Bad news: You *will* run into problems at college. Good news: You'll be on the campus at a time when colleges and universities are sensitive as never before to the difficulties students encounter. You won't have to deal with your academic, physical, legal, social, economic, or emotional problems entirely alone. Your task, though, is to develop the skill of knowing when it's time to seek help, where to find it, and what to ask for when you get there.

 ## What happens if I get sick?

 Most colleges and universities generally provide at minimal cost such benefits as unlimited visits to the campus infirmary for consultation and treatment by health service doctors and nurses, routine diagnostic tests and X rays, first-aid treatment of injuries not requiring surgery, commonly used medicines, psychological counseling for personal and emotional problems, and in some cases, even allergy shots and immunizations.

What your campus health service probably will not cover is the cost of such items as visits to private physicians or private health-care facilities, house calls, surgery and hospitalization, eye examinations and treatments, contraceptives, obstetrical care, and treatment for illnesses or injuries suffered while you are out of town or on holidays.

Your college also will make available a supplemental health insurance plan to cover hospital care and various other medical services not routinely provided for you on campus. You'll be urged to sign up for this additional coverage (it may cost you about $200 or so a year) unless you show that you're already covered by your parents' medical insurance program.

The extent of on-campus services routinely available will vary from one college to another, as will the amount of the health service fee. In general, however, you can count on prompt, reliable, and inexpensive health care while you're in college.

The doctors, incidentally, have become specialists in treating health problems of young people, and they're usually good at what they do. "The campus is an upbeat kind of place," one university physician reported, explaining why he had chosen it over private practice. "Also, it's incredibly rare for us to ever lose a patient here. I like that."

What if I need emergency dental care?

A Some colleges and universities include dental care as part of their student health service package. Most, however, do not; they expect you to solve your dental problems in your own way.

It's a good idea, then, to promptly establish a relationship with a dentist in your college community. If you've already become known as a patient—say you've been in for your six-month checkup and cleaning—you'll feel free to call upon your college-town dentist if you have an emergency. Ask local students, your dorm director, or your faculty adviser to recommend a good dentist whose office is near the campus. Your campus health service or the county dental society, if there is one, can provide some names for you also. Larger communities will have one or more emergency dental clinics, and the yellow pages may list private dentists who are available to see patients on a round-the-clock basis.

If your college or university has its own dental school, you may want to use its clinic. Treatments are handled by advanced dental students, under the careful supervision of their professors. There are some disadvantages to having your work done at a dental school clinic; waiting periods are sometimes longer, and the student clinic may not be open on the days you need it. On the other hand, the techniques used are among the most sophisticated, and the costs are only a fraction of those charged by dentists in private practice.

Q How often and under what circumstances will the college be in touch with my family?

A Unless you're involved in a genuine medical emergency, your parents might never be contacted directly by your college or university (except to be invited to Parents' Day or something equally innocuous). At one time, college officials would mail your grade forms directly to your family, along with other ghastly messages, such as a notice that you had been placed on academic probation or that several books were overdue at the library. This doesn't happen much anymore. Fearful of the new privacy statutes, the larger institutions, and especially those that are state supported, have become extremely cautious about releasing information to anyone except the individual student concerned. At some schools you may sign a release form authorizing the college to mail your grades and related messages home. Otherwise, your grade reports and other official communications will be dispatched directly to you. Whether you share this information with your parents, says the university, is your business.

At some private schools, however, and especially at the smaller ones, efforts continue to make parents fully aware of the educational progress of their sons and daughters. This means if you make the dean's list—or if you get busted for possession—your folks may get a letter about it.

Q What if my grades start slipping?

A The first step, an obvious one but often overlooked, is for you to do some no-nonsense self-analysis as to *why* your grades are going down. The answer you get will suggest the most direct means of attacking the problem. If, for example, your grades are in a tailspin because of an emotional problem—depression, say, or anxiety or insecurity—then by all means make an appointment with a college counselor and talk it out.

If the material in your courses is fairly standard stuff, but you just aren't getting it—math, foreign languages, and some sciences set off this kind of confusion—your best solution may be simply to arrange for one or more private tutors to get you back on the track. On the other hand, if the difficulty comes in interpreting the material—this happens frequently in humanities courses—then you should try getting to know your professor better. Request an appointment and let him or her know you have a problem and, more important, that you're concerned about it. Some professors do their best teaching in individual conferences with their students.

Finally, if your self-analysis indicates that you're headed for trouble because you can't or won't spend enough time studying, then you might need to rethink your priorities and analyze the way you're presently carving up your days and nights. In other words, you may need to take a leave of absence from the staff of the school newspaper, cut back your seven-dates-a-week social life, unload a time-consuming office in your fraternity, or even drop a course if it's about to drag your other courses and you down with it.

The important thing, obviously, is to do something now. Don't hold off until finals, when it's too late for the professor or your faculty adviser to do anything for you. Professors aren't much impressed with students who wait until the last day of classes to ask for help.

So far, we've been describing a situation in which you can tell your grades are actually slipping. There's another problem, one more difficult to deal with, and that is when there are no grades until the final exam, when it's all or nothing. Many courses are run this way. You may think you're understanding the material as you go along, but you aren't sure. In that case, you need to create your own feedback. So every few days ask yourself (1) If the final exam in this course were held today, what questions would most likely be asked? (2) How well could I answer them? Your answers to these questions will indicate whether you need to pursue one or more of the steps outlined above.

Q. If I need assistance in a specific course, how can I find a tutor? How much does tutoring cost?

A. Start by checking with the department secretary. Chances are he or she has a list of students who are willing and able to tutor, along with their individual rates. You can then make your own arrangements. The prices are usually quite reasonable. Student tutoring fees begin as low as $5 an hour. Off-campus professional tutoring offices, staffed by experienced teachers, charge more. Their services are usually advertised in student newspapers and on circulars posted in the library, student union, dorm, or other strategic spots around the campus. Many problems, however, the kinds you encounter in freshman French or college algebra, can be solved with help from a student tutor in a few hours' time, and for about the cost of dinner and a movie.

Q. What help is available for "math-anxious" students?

A. Millions of Americans suffer from some form of math anxiety. They are intimidated by the subject and avoid it whenever possible. In this computer age, however, it's becoming increasingly more difficult to get through college without some understanding of mathematics, which means more and more students must begin coming to terms with their math anxieties.

Many counseling centers offer some sort of assistance. One approach is to organize volunteer math-anxious students into informal support groups where students can talk out their fears and frustrations and begin to deal with them. Under the guidance of professional counselors, the students may then be given simple math problems to solve slowly and without pressure. Eventually, for an encouraging number of students, the math anxiety is either whipped outright or brought under sufficient control to see them through the math portions of their undergraduate courses.

Q. How can I overcome this problem I have with procrastination?

A. Jokes on this subject abound ("Procrastination is ruining me and I'm going to do something about it—one of these days!"), but the students who are affected by it aren't laughing. Procrastination is terribly commonplace among undergraduates (and throughout all of society, for that matter) and it probably accounts for more bad grades and, worse yet, more anxiety than just about any other single academic problem.

All of us prefer to put things off at times, certainly, but serious procrastinators can postpone themselves into scholarly oblivion. Students with perfectionist tendencies seem especially vulnerable; they keep delaying work on a project until they finally find themselves overwhelmed by it.

Procrastination frequently reflects a deeper emotional problem, such as resentment of authority (as symbolized by deadlines) or a longing to have more control over one's own life. In other cases, procrastination stems from a fear of failure or even a fear of success ("if I do well on this paper, I'll just put more pressure on myself to keep doing well on all the others"). If your procrastination has become an entrenched life habit, then you need to see a counselor about ways to deal with it.

In most instances, however, procrastination is simply a management problem. The procrastinator needs to learn how to analyze the tasks ahead and carve them up into workable short-term objectives that can be attained one day at a time. Suppose, for example, you've got a test in freshman English next week on *King Lear*. You've leafed through the play, only to become thoroughly intimidated by the enormity and power of that drama. *Don't panic*—and don't procrastinate. Instead of muttering "I've got to read *King Lear* today," give yourself an easier, more manageable goal: "Today, I'm going to read Act I of *King Lear.*" Then do it, pat yourself on the back for attaining a worthy objective, and go on with the rest of your life. Your success with Act I will reinforce you for tomorrow, when you tackle Act II. By the end of the week, you'll have had the time and generated the momentum to read all five acts; your next day's task might be to review the work, place the characters in context, and anticipate questions your prof might ask. You and the Bard will be well acquainted by now, and you'll have won a series of impressive victories over your procrastination.

The same divide-and-conquer philosophy applies to the papers you have to write. Don't, for heaven's sake, hold off writing until you've thought up the perfect opening sentences. Just get something down on paper, even if it's only a barely coherent smattering of phrases, sentence fragments, and ideas you think are pertinent. Those first thoughts probably won't be elegantly expressed, but at least they provide a point of departure, something you can look at, coordinate, analyze, polish, and add to in subsequent revisions. Unless there's a crisis, don't try to write the whole essay at once; set a reasonable goal for today (three pages of a first draft, for example) and forge ahead. You'll get there.

Your college counseling office is used to answering questions about procrastination, so don't hesitate to seek professional help if you need it. Often the counselors will conduct workshops devoted to this subject, and you might want to sign up for one of these. Procrastination workshops are often free or available at minimal cost, and in five or six study sessions you can pick up useful insights into task and time management. You'll also find that a great many other students are coping with procrastination problems and that your own situation is by no means uncommon.

Q What provisions do colleges make for handicapped students?

A It took a lot of years, with a lot of heartbreak during the wait, but there is now a clear federal regulation aimed at ending the injustice and demeaning hassles affecting handicapped students. This law, Section 504 of the Rehabilitation Act of 1973, says that "No otherwise qualified handicapped individual in the United States . . . shall, solely by reason of his or her handicap, be excluded from the participation in, be denied the benefits of, or be subjected to discrimination under any program or activity receiving federal financial assistance." Since your college or university almost certainly receives federal aid, the chances are excellent that massive efforts are being made to comply with the law. Mention the possible loss of federal money to a college president, and you immediately receive his or her earnest and undivided attention.

Section 504 does not require that every building or every part of a building be accessible to handicapped persons, just that the program as a whole must be accessible. Some older classroom buildings may not yet have the ramps, elevators, and installations needed to accommodate students in wheelchairs. But if a handicapped student is assigned to a building that still has architectural barriers in it, then (1) he or she must be reassigned to a comparable class in a building that is accessible, (2) the entire class must be moved to an accessible location, or (3) some other means must be employed, such as arranging to have the course material taught to the handicapped student at home. This last alternative is clearly the least preferable. It is far better, educationally, to integrate the handicapped student into the class rather than deliver the course content to the student.

While there is much work left to be done, most institutions have devoted a great deal of energy and money toward making their campuses accessible through ramps, curb cuts, and remodeled restroom facilities. Many schools also employ specially trained teachers to work with students who have speech or hearing handicaps, and many college libraries now have available sophisticated magnifying equipment and a whole range of audiotapes to assist students with severely impaired vision.

At larger schools there might be a handicapped students' office (it may be called the Office of Equal Opportunity) to provide information and support. Each academic department should have a faculty or staff member designated to deal with specific concerns of handicapped students—matters such as provisions for special exams, course scheduling, and classroom changes. The names of these individuals probably will be announced during orientation, but if not, the office of the dean of students will have them. And, if you want to know in more detail what rights handicapped persons have under federal law so that you can judge how well your college or university complies with them, read Section 504 of the Rehabilitation Act of 1973.

Q What can I do if I am the victim of sexual harassment or discrimination?

A Whether consciously or unconsciously motivated, sexual harassment does occur throughout society, and college professors, who should know better, are not infrequently at fault. Sex discrimination can take many forms. For example, your professor may not regard your career goals seriously, believing them to be unsuitable for members of your sex. You may be subjected to pressure by a professor to participate with him or her in social and/or sexual activities. Perhaps you don't get a fair shot at financial aid, admission to a program, or some other academic benefit for sexist reasons. Or you may find that the material in your course (lectures or textbook) demeans you because of your sex.

If you are discriminated against or harassed, you may well feel helpless and alone. No need to. The law is on your side, and there are people on your campus, such as affirmative action officers, who can help.

Following is a list of specific options open to you if you are victimized by sex discrimination. These steps are adapted from a statement issued by the Utah State University Commission on the Status of Women and reported in that school's orientation book. They apply to campuses everywhere and, as warranted, they should be carried out in this order:

1. Talk to the professor. Explain why you consider the particular action or comment as sexist. Individuals are often unaware of how their remarks can hurt. (This analogy might be useful: Would you make fun of a person's skin color or religion? Then why do so with sex?) In many cases, simply raising the consciousness of the offender might help him or her avoid careless, perhaps unintentional, sexism in the future.

2. Contact relevant campus authorities. Virtually every college has an affirmative action officer (usually a faculty member or staff person appointed for a given term). Your academic dean knows what the law says about sex discrimination, and so does your dean of students. These individuals will listen to you and provide help and advice.

3. Put your complaint in writing. If you have talked to the professor and sex discrimination continues, write a letter to him or her outlining the specific incidents and explain why they offend you. Send a carbon of your letter to the professor's department chairman, to your dean, and to your campus affirmative action officer. That should get some results. In addition, you can write out your complaints in your student evaluation of the course if your school provides this option. These comments will be read by deans and department heads and taken into account in determining the professor's yearly performance rating.

4. File a formal grievance. This is a serious step—virtually a legal proceeding—and should not be undertaken without thought, discussion, and counsel.

The overwhelming majority of discrimination cases can be corrected without ever going beyond Step 1. Old prejudices are fast disappearing on most campuses, and the climate today is far healthier than it has ever been. But *any* sex discrimination is too much and if it happens to you, you should know you have the means at hand to fight back.

 Is legal assistance available for students?

AMany colleges and universities retain an attorney to visit the campus several hours each week to answer legal questions that students have. Contact the office of the dean of students for details.

The federally funded Legal Services office in your area can provide civil, but not criminal, legal assistance to students whose income is sufficiently low to qualify for this free service. The criteria used for determining need are constantly being reviewed and may change, but, generally, if you live away from your parents and your income is less than $4600 a year, you may be eligible for help from Legal Services.

If you want to hire a lawyer and don't know how to find one, consult your telephone directory for the number of your local or state bar association. Someone there will assist you by matching your particular need with the type of law practiced by one or more attorneys nearby.

Various advocacy groups may also be able to help. The Better Business Bureau, for example, takes complaints of unfair business practice and serves as a clearinghouse for consumer information about questionable companies or activities. The local or national chapter of the American Civil Liberties Union is especially vigilant in matters involving discrimination and freedom of speech, religion, and assembly. Your state Attorney General's office may operate a Consumer Protection Agency to investigate questionable business practices.

If you need assistance with an academically related problem—if you've been verbally abused by a teacher, for example, or you've been wrongfully accused of cheating—then find out if your college or university has an ombudsman. On many larger campuses, an ombudsman conducts impartial investigations into student complaints, and the findings—as professors and administrators can tell you—are listened to with great respect. The ombudsman is usually a senior, tenured member of the faculty who has been asked to serve a year or two in that delicate position. (The term ombudsman is Swedish, and it was originally used to describe an official who investigates complaints against public officials.)

Working independently of the college administration and all other groups on the campus, the ombudsman seeks to combat injustice and resolve conflicts. Students can communicate with their ombudsman in confidence. Though the ombudsman does not have the power to reverse decisions or to punish people, he or she does have the ability—and the clout—to raise hell in the students' behalf, and that is usually enough.

 What help is available for dealing with emotional problems?

A While faculty members can provide a great deal of assistance in certain areas—suggestions regarding career opportunities, academic procedures and regulations, books to read and courses to take—they won't necessarily be able to help you with emotional difficulties.

On most campuses, trained psychologists and counselors are on hand to help students solve personal, academic, and vocational problems. Students typically experience feelings of depression, emotional insecurity, and anxiety at various points throughout their college careers; some have difficulty relating to parents and peers or in adjusting to the new environment. The counseling staff is there to lend an ear.

Since the counseling offices are funded by the institution, there is normally no charge for the counseling itself. The counseling is confidential, of course, and purely voluntary. Students are not required to visit the counseling office, but many of them do avail themselves of this sensitive and valuable service.

Q What do I do if I suspect my roommate or friend has anorexia or bulimia?

A Whether the condition is anorexia nervosa (a disorder in which the person, terrified of being or becoming fat, refuses to eat much of anything at all and begins literally wasting away) or bulimia (the binge-purge disease in which one gorges huge amounts of food, then either vomits or takes laxatives to avoid gaining weight), your roommate or friend needs professional treatment. You are neither medically qualified nor emotionally equipped to deal with a depressive condition of this magnitude and complexity.

Once rare, anorexia and bulimia are now being diagnosed on campuses across the country. Medical experts estimate that as many as 7 million women will suffer symptoms of bulimia at some point in their lives; college counselors believe that as many as 10 percent of the coeds on some campuses are bulimic. (The incidence is far lower among men.) And while the victims might look healthy, they probably suffer from internal disorders and are prone to other psychological disturbances, which frequently manifest themselves in suicide and alcohol and drug abuse. Both diseases, in other words, can be deadly.

First, urge your roommate or friend to seek professional care. If that entreaty doesn't work, then notify your resident adviser and, if it becomes serious, the counseling center or health clinic. If your roommate will not get help, you may want to move to a different room. If this sounds callous, you should realize that the alternative—trying to live with someone who urgently requires treatment—will almost surely be bad for both of you. Those for whom staying thin is an illness usually don't make good roommates. Their frequent, uncontrollable urge for food often leads them to steal from others, roommates included. Worst of all is the emotional damage they intentionally or unintentionally inflict on those around them. "Every time I look up," says one coed of her bulimic roommate, "I see this human being in need of help."

In extreme cases, the treatment may require hospitalization; under tightly controlled conditions, the patient gradually learns to eat normally. Antidepressant drugs have worked well, as have some attempts by psychologists to get at the emotional causes of the problem and to rebuild the patient's self esteem. In any event, a person suffering from anorexia or bulimia needs professional attention, and you might too if you try to cope alone with a situation that could lead to a devastating outcome.

Q What is AIDS? Are the stories about AIDS exaggerated? What can I do to avoid catching it?

AIDS is Acquired Immune Deficiency Syndrome, a virus that knocks out the body's ability to fight infections, ultimately leaving the victim powerless when attacked by illnesses that otherwise would be thrown off easily. The impact of AIDS is hard to overestimate; some regard the disease as the plague of the eighties.

According to figures released in April 1988 by the National Centers for Disease Control, some 57,575 cases of AIDS had been reported in the United States. Already more than 32,000, or slightly more than half, have died from a disease that was virtually unheard of before 1981. Some researchers predict that more than 291,000 Americans will have contracted AIDS by the end of 1991 and that perhaps as many as 180,000 persons will have died of it by then. The disease has no known cure.

In a recent interview with the *New York Times,* Dr. Beverlie Conant Sloane, director of health education at Dartmouth College, warned that "some students think they are invulnerable. Some think they are not susceptible to getting AIDS at a time when the Disease Control Center is predicting that AIDS will be the number one killer on campus by 1991."

If you are sexually active, doctors insist that it is not only important but critical that you be informed as you make decisions that can affect not only your health but also your life.

The human immunodeficiency virus (HIV), which causes AIDS, is spread through sexual contact when infected body fluids (notably semen and blood) are introduced into the body of another person. In this country, AIDS is passed along most commonly (63 percent) by homosexual or bisexual men (through oral and anal sex) and among drug users who share contaminated needles (18 percent). Transfusions of infected blood account for about 3 percent of AIDS cases, a figure that should decrease dramatically as better blood testing procedures continue to be developed.

AIDS can also be transmitted during sexual intercourse from women to men as the virus exists in the cervical and vaginal fluids of infected women. (In Africa, almost as many women as men are AIDS victims.) The heterosexual cases in the United States in mid-1988 numbered 2,285 (4 percent).

In other words, researchers tell us, certain groups of persons are much more likely to become infected with AIDS:

- Homosexual males (not involved in monogamous relationships) and bisexual males
- IV (intravenous) drug users
- Prostitutes, both male and female
- Any man or woman who has, or has had, many sex partners
- Any man or woman who has contracted other sexually transmitted diseases

"If I'm careful and practice safe sex and use protective devices," you may be telling yourself, "I won't get AIDS." That may oversimplify the situation to a dangerous degree. Many persons, college students included, have been led by persons in positions of authority to conclude that devices such as condoms and spermicides offer complete protection. Indeed, condom dispensing machines are making their appearances on more and more college campuses (to the astonishment of more than one member of the Board of Trustees and probably some parents as well). At Dartmouth last year, for example, students at registration could pick up, along with their class cards, a kit that included a condom, a tube of lubricant jelly, a dental dam for oral sex, and a brutally explicit pamphlet explaining how to have safer sex in the era of AIDS.

In his excellent book, *Safe Sex in a Dangerous World,* Dr. Art Ulene declares that " 'truly safe sex' is an all-or-nothing thing. Sex is either 100 percent safe or it's not, even when it's 'almost safe.' If you can't find a safe partner (one who has never been infected with the AIDS virus), don't kid yourself into believing that there is a perfectly safe alternative—other than abstinence."

Condoms, as Dr. Ulene and others have pointed out, are not perfect. They may be put on incorrectly, they can slip off, they can tear or break or leak. A number of women whose partners use condoms for birth control purposes nevertheless become pregnant (the estimates can run as high as 10 percent); it follows that the same ratio of condom users for AIDS-prevention purposes is similarly at risk.

Promiscuity increases the odds against you. If abstinence is not an acceptable choice, then it is essential that you use protective devices, avoid anal sex (the tissues in the anus are thinner and crack open more easily), and limit your exposure to partners with a very low risk of AIDS infection. And, although it has become a cliché to say so, bear in mind that you are not just having sex with your partner; you are sleeping with all the other people your partner has ever slept with. You take on their histories, reflecting their previous decisions, some of which may have been most unwise. You could pay dearly for someone else's miscalculation, not just your own. Until there is a cure—and the AIDS virus continues to baffle the brightest minds the world medical community has studying it—then condoms and safe partners are good defenses, and abstinence is the best defense of all.

Q How do you treat people who have AIDS? What if my roommate tests HIV positive?

AAIDS is not passed along via casual contact, and most researchers agree that it is not easy to transmit this virus from one person to another through nonsexual contact. You do not, they say, pick it up from food prepared by someone with AIDS or through drinking glasses or dishes. The virus itself cannot live long outside the human body (without precisely the right conditions being present) and is readily killed by heat and alcohol and contact with other solutions, such as bleach.

Careful studies of persons sharing the same household as a family member with AIDS turn up no evidence that the virus could be spread by hugging, kissing, sharing of bathroom and kitchen facilities, and other close, but nonsexual, contact. Nor has it been proven that mosquitos can spread the disease.

Yet there remains the terrible dread of AIDS that can cause us to shrink away from any association with a victim. Most of the fears are ignorant and unfounded, but they exist. (Indeed, a worried faculty colleague of mine was at one time anxious to propose a policy change that would protect professors from having to teach, in a classroom, a student with AIDS. Fortunately, the fellow was soon persuaded that the virus is not known ever to have been passed along during an academic discussion.)

In time, no doubt, there will be a vaccine developed that can conquer AIDS. Until then, we have no reason to avoid casual contact with persons who test HIV positive (many of whom will never develop AIDS symptoms). Meanwhile, we can be hopeful and supportive to those we care about, knowing that they are engaged in a fearsome personal and medical struggle.

Q What if my roommate becomes depressed to the point of mentioning suicide?

A This may be an attempt to gain attention, and it is almost certainly a cry for help. It's also too much responsibility for you to attempt to handle on your own. Professional counseling is urgently needed, and it is available. Virtually every campus has access to highly trained psychologists and/or psychiatrists who can help students begin to get at the *why* of their depression.

If your roommate won't seek help voluntarily, then you should alert the counseling center and/or health clinic in your roommate's behalf. It would be better for your relationship if you got permission first, though obviously this is a secondary consideration: "Look, roomie, you need to see a professional about your problem. Now if you don't make the call, I will. I don't want you to think I'm finking on you, but this is just too important to ignore."

Q Is there religious life on campus?

A This question, or some form of it, is frequently raised by parents and grandparents who darkly suspect that it must be easier to push a camel through the eye of a needle than it is to lure a college student into the pews on the Sabbath.

I won't pretend that campuses are islands of unrelieved virtue, but they aren't Sodom and Gomorrah, either, and the fact is that there are splendid opportunities for religious fellowship at most schools. And increasing numbers of students are taking advantage of them.

"Student involvement with us is on the upswing, and students are more serious about their religion," one Protestant minister explained. "They may not spend as much time with us as they'd like to—more students have jobs now, and they don't have as much free time—but the quality of their interest is stronger now than it's been in some years."

Part of this may be attributable to a widespread return to traditional values generally, but campus ministers think a quest for identity may be involved also. "It's more than just the 'Me Generation' thing," one youth minister explained. "It's an attempt to find personal meaning in a highly competitive society."

Most major religious faiths have established a presence on, or very near, the campus. Larger church units, such as the Methodist Wesley Foundation, may maintain their own quarters, complete with chapel, recreational facilities, kitchen, seminar rooms, and so on. But even denominations with only a handful of students can usually arrange to schedule regular worship services, perhaps using one of the meeting rooms in the student union building.

One of the most extensive campus ministries is the Roman Catholic Newman Center, which, near the campus where I work, operates in effect a self-contained parish church. The staff includes 3 priests, 2 nuns, and 2 highly trained students who act as peer ministers. The Newman Center conducts Mass each day and sponsors a wide range of other activities, such as parties, classes, discussion meetings, and an inexpensive spaghetti supper on weekends (when campus dining rooms are closed).

In another large campus organization, the Baptist Student Union, the emphasis is on weekday fellowship, the idea being that the BSU should serve as a link to the "regular" churches downtown or back home. The campus BSU does schedule a number of worship meetings and Bible study sessions, a midweek prayer service, seminars, retreats, and the like, but it is also a social organization, vigorously engaged in intramural sports, service projects, community activities, suppers, and parties. The BSU minister's records show that about 8,000 Baptist students are enrolled on this particular campus; on a given Sunday, about 1,000 of these attend local Baptist churches, and an estimated 500 more students go home for the weekend and attend church services in their local communities. These attendance figures would compare, certainly, with those of the country as a whole.

The youth ministers I've known are bright, well-educated, generally unflappable individuals, capable of sustaining enthusiasm through long and wildly irregular hours, and—best of all—they are sensitive to the concerns of young people who are just entering new stages of independence, experimentation, and uncertainty. Campus youth ministers mostly listen. Sometimes they talk. Rarely do they pontificate.

"Often we're dealing with impatient young people who see things in stark terms of black and white," one articulate youth minister, a priest, told me. "They point out that the Church itself doesn't have its own act together—and sometimes it doesn't. Their longing for quick and simple solutions can at times make them vulnerable to groups that promise easy, permanent, black-and-white answers. I try to get them to be patient, to appreciate the wait, and to have the courage to take steps into the world of shades of gray."

CHAPTER 6

PAYING FOR IT ALL

Money problems have waylaid more college careers than laziness and stupidity combined. A college education costs thousands of dollars. In most cases, the minimum payback on that investment, expressed in terms of increased earning power over a lifetime, comes in the *tens* of thousands of dollars. But that rosy long-term prospect isn't much comfort when the bills for tuition, fees, and room and board are "due and payable." "It used to be that 'a fool and his money are soon parted,' " grumbled a student of mine. "Now it seems that *everybody* and his money are soon parted."

In managing money—as with managing time and energy—the shrewdest students are the shrewdest planners, those who work hard contriving ways to get the best use of what they have. This chapter won't make you rich, but it can help you plan better.

 How much money will I need for living expenses?

First of all, you need to estimate the costs *not* provided for in such big-ticket items as room, board, and tuition. For example, your dining card may not cover meals on the weekends. And you may not always get back to the dorm before the cafeteria closes. Or you may get halfway through the serving line and suffer a massive craving for junk food. ("One more balanced, nourishing, color-coordinated meal and I'll scream!"). In other words, you'll probably eat out several times each month. Tuition payments also won't take care of such items as lab fees for specific courses, late registration charges, drop-and-add fees, library fines, and a gang of other course-related hits your budget will have to absorb. Individually, these fees may not amount to much, but over the span of a year they can easily reach $250 or more.

Figure in some expenses for transportation. (That item alone can run to $1000 or more for an out-of-state student who visits home a few times a year from a distant campus. In-state students, on the average, spend an estimated $250 a semester, $500 a year, on transportation costs.) Even if you don't have a car, you'll find yourself buying gas occasionally for someone who does. Besides trips to see your folks, you probably will want to spend some out-of-town weekends visiting friends, attending ball games, whatever. Your long-distance telephone bills, unless you're always able to call collect, will amount to several dollars a month more than you think.

If you're in a fraternity or sorority, you can expect a number of extra expenses throughout the year, mostly connected with entertaining. These include special assessments to cover your share of parties and dances, gifts, photographs, and other memorabilia—sometimes totaling $500 or more a year in addition to your monthly dues.

You'll also need to cover the cost of such items as toothpaste, deodorant, shampoo, laundry expenses—all the things you got free while you lived with your parents but must now handle by yourself.

Socializing, even of the most temperate variety, is expensive. One movie a week, one half a pizza a week, one soft drink and one candy bar a day—and you've shelled out over $50 a month. And this describes life somewhere well this side of the fast lane. Splurge on a rock concert or a football weekend and you're talking big-time expenditures.

So how much money will you need? Colleges and universities are understandably reluctant to become too specific on this one. At the University of South Carolina, as an example of a state school, the 1988 estimate for personal expenses (books were counted separately) was $1413 a year.

Colleges' estimates are probably low. Not intentionally, but low because they fail to include all the expenses students realistically incur. My own feeling is that you should expect to spend close to $1800 a year for personal expenses. That's $200 a month for nine months, which is certainly not lavish, but probably adequate. Plan on less and you may have to borrow. If you should come in under that amount, then you can always plow your savings into next year's budget.

Q How much will my textbooks cost?

A Book prices have gone up enormously, but even so they account for only a tiny fraction—no more than 5 percent, and possibly far less—of your total college expenses. Depending on your field of study and other factors, you should average about $350 a year for books and supplies. In some fields, sciences and certain professional areas, the total can easily run higher.

You can reduce that figure somewhat by selling your books at the end of the term; you won't get the full price back, by any means, but you can recover at least a portion of the costs. You can also save by purchasing used books when they're available. (A tip: Used books are gobbled up fast, so buy early. This, in turn, requires you to sign up for advising and preregistration appointments as soon as possible so you'll know what courses you'll be taking. If you register late, you're unlikely to find used books available.)

Also be sure to find out whether each book on your course list is required or recommended. If a book is merely recommended, you may be able to get along without it. Bookstores are supposed to label these distinctions plainly, but they don't always do so; if you're uncertain, ask a clerk to check in the office for a copy of the professor's ordering instructions. Some professors put copies of the books on their list on reserve at the library; if this happens on your campus you may be able to avoid buying some books altogether, though it's pretty chancy to assume you'll be able to gain access to the books at the reserve room precisely when you need them most.

Q What types of financial aid are available?

A large percentage of students—40 percent on some campuses, far more on others—receive financial aid from a variety of sources. The amount of support you can get will be based to a great extent on the reports provided to the colleges you're interested in by one of two nationwide financial need analysis services. The College Scholarship Service's Financial Aid Form (FAF) is generally required of those students who took the College Board's SATs. It is obtainable from high school guidance counselors, college financial aid officers, or the College Scholarship Service, Box CN 6341, Princeton, New Jersey 08541.

The American College Testing Program's counterpart to CSS's Financial Aid Form is the Family Financial Statement (FFS); this form is generally used by those colleges that require applicants to submit ACT scores. Check with participating-college financial aid officers for the appropriate forms or write to ACT Student Assistance Program, 2201 North Dodge Street, P.O. Box 1000, Iowa City, Iowa 52243. (Note well: as you will have discovered by now, different schools utilize different forms, analysis services, and procedures. Make sure you know what *each* school you're applying to expects.)

On both the FAF and the FFS, you and your parents will be asked to provide information about your assets, liabilities, annual income, and expenses. The figures you and your family send in will be evaluated by impartial, professional analysts, and the CSS or ACT will then send the colleges and universities you are interested in attending a confidential report containing an estimate of how much money you and your family can reasonably be expected to contribute toward the cost of your education.

In the meantime, each of these schools will be computing a student expense budget, which includes tuition and fees, charges for room and board, an estimate of personal expenses, and even travel costs for students who live far away. Your need for financial aid is understood to be the difference between the college's student expense budget and the need analysis service's estimate of how much you and your family can be expected to pay.

For example, say you're considering two colleges. One of these, Siwash, estimates its yearly costs per student to be $11,800. The CSS evaluation of your Financial Aid Form projects that you and your family should be able to pay $6500. Siwash would then consider your "demonstrated financial need" to be $5300—the amount of help you'll need to make it there.

The other school you're interested in, Samson State, is publicly supported, and the individual student costs are far less, an estimated $6500 a year. The CSS, again, estimates that your family can and should be able to pay up to $6500, so your "demonstrated financial need" at Samson State would be zero. We will discuss your own contribution, and your family's, later in this chapter.

At most schools, actual need is the primary or often the *only* basis for awarding financial aid. Other colleges may take into account your academic potential as reflected in your high school class rank, SAT or ACT scores, and so on, in attempting to determine the extent of financial support.

In addition to filing the FAF or the FFS, which you should do as soon as possible after January 1 of your senior year, you will need to apply for financial aid directly to the college or colleges you're interested in attending. Your application for financial aid, by the way, normally will not be a factor in your admission; most college and university admissions officers make their decision on the basis of your academic qualifications alone, and not on how much money you and your family can muster.

Your college's offer of financial aid, if and when it comes, will most probably be presented in the form of a "package" consisting of some combination of grant and scholarship money, a student loan, and a part-time job under the College Work-Study Program. Here are some of the components that make up financial aid packages:

GRANTS AND SCHOLARSHIPS

Pell Grants. Formerly called Basic Educational Opportunity Grants, these are federal grants awarded to undergraduates from lower-income families. (Families with somewhat larger incomes may qualify for Pell Grants if several children are in college at once.) A grant is a gift—money you don't have to pay back. You can apply for a Pell Grant by completing the appropriate section of the FAF and/or the FFS. These awards can range up to $2200 a year.

Supplemental Educational Opportunity Grants (SEOG). These are federal funds awarded to undergraduate students who have exceptional financial need. These can be as much as $4000 a year.

State grants. Many states now provide tuition assistance to their residents who qualify. Your high school guidance counselor or college financial aid officer can fill you in on the specific terms, which vary from year to year and from state to state.

College and university scholarships. These are grants from the school's own endowed funds awarded on the basis of academic potential and/or financial need.

Restricted scholarships. These funds have specific limitations imposed by the people who donated the money. A scholarship might be set up, for example, to support a student from Appalachia who wants to study chemical engineering or a student of Hispanic descent who was a champion debater in high school. There are literally thousands of these scholarships, a number of which go unclaimed each year simply because there are no qualified candidates for them. Your college financial aid officers will study your credentials carefully and automatically consider you for any scholarships for which you might qualify. It's in your best interests, however, to double-check the list of scholarships offered by your college and request specifically that you be nominated for those for which you may be eligible.

Minority scholarships. Special scholarship funds have been established on many campuses for minority students with a high level of need. These go well beyond federal and state grant support, so if you are a member of a minority group and have demonstrated financial need, make certain you are considered.

Special scholarships and grants. These include the scholarships provided by the Army, Navy/Marine Corps, and Air Force ROTC programs as well as privately financed merit scholarships that are based on specific accomplishments in a given field, such as sports, music, or foreign language study rather than on financial need. Many colleges offer their own merit scholarships, but there are also numerous national competitions open to students with the appropriate experience and talents. Check with your high school guidance counselor or college financial aid officer for detailed information about merit scholarships for which you might be eligible.

STUDENT LOANS

Perkins Loans. Once referred to as National Direct Student Loans, Perkins Loans provide substantial chunks of money—up to $4500 for your first two years of college or a total of $9000 for a complete undergraduate program of study ($18,000 is the limit for undergraduate plus graduate study) at highly favorable interest rates, currently 5 percent. Repayment begins nine months *after* you graduate, leave school, or drop below half-time student status. To qualify, you must demonstrate financial need and sign a promissory note. Under certain conditions (you serve in the Peace Corps or VISTA or the military, for example), your Perkins Loan repayments could be deferred. And if you become a teacher in what has been officially designated as a disadvantaged area, part or all of your loan may be cancelled. The conditions for these loans change from time to time, but as a general rule most students who qualify for financial aid also qualify for:

Stafford Student Loans. Formerly known as Guaranteed Students Loans, these are administered through local banks and credit unions, and the re-payment terms are favorable: 8 percent interest for the first five years of re-payment and 10 percent after that. Undergraduates with demonstrated financial need may be eligible to borrow up to $2625 for each of their freshman and sophomore years, $4000 for each of three additional years of undergraduate study, and $7500 a year as graduate students (with a total borrowing limit of $54,750 for undergraduate and graduate study) To apply, pick up a Stafford Student Loan form from a lending agency. Your home-town bank may be one; if not, someone there can refer you to the nearest savings and loan, bank, or credit union that participates in this program. After you complete your portion of the application, send the form to the col-lege or university where you intend to use the money. The school's financial aid officer will verify your eligibility to enroll as well as the costs of a year of study there and will report your demonstrated financial need. He or she then returns the application to you, and you send it to the lending agency, which disburses the amount of the loan to the college or university. Your Stafford Student Loan repayments begin six months after you graduate, quit school, or drop below half-time status.

Insured supplementary loans. These include SLS loans, for students, and PLUS loans, for your parents. Like Stafford Loans, these come from lending agencies such as local banks or credit unions. However, a PLUS or SLS loan repayment schedule begins within 60 days. The interest rates can be ad-justed each year; for the 1987–88 academic year, the rate was pegged at 10.27 percent. PLUS and SLS loans do not require you to demonstrate finan-cial need. As with Stafford Loans, there may be an origination fee of up to 5.5 percent of the loan principal—money charged by the agency in your state that guarantees the loan.

Institutional loans. A number of colleges and universities have available low-interest loan funds established by friends and alumni. These loans may be restricted to students in certain fields of study.

STUDENT EMPLOYMENT

College Work-Study Program. This is a federally funded jobs program for students who can prove financial need. Students who receive Work-Study assignments typically put in 10 to 15 hours a week as assistants in campus libraries, academic departments, research labs, or off-campus nonprofit agencies, and they can earn $700 to $1500 during the academic year (in some cases more).

Other work opportunities. Many students, whether or not they are eligible for financial aid, land part-time and/or co-op jobs on and off the campus. (See pp. 137–38.)

Your financial aid package, then, might include some scholarship or grant money, which you don't have to pay back; a loan, which you do have to repay, but on favorable terms and not immediately; and a part-time job.

Financial aid for college students is an extraordinarily complicated business (see box), and the circumstances at individual colleges around the country are constantly changing. To make sure your information is both complete and current, check with both your high school guidance counselor and the financial aid officer of each college you're considering. And bear in mind this important point: If you are qualified to attend a particular college, and if you and your family are prepared to assume a reasonable share of the costs of your education, then the college may well be able to help you with the rest.

Financial Aid Glossary

The terminology used by financial aid directors can be bewildering. Here's a brief glossary to help you understand it:

ACT: The American College Testing Program, administrator of one of the large financial aid need analysis services. Headquartered in Iowa City, Iowa, ACT evaluates information provided by you on the FFS to determine how much money you and your family can afford to contribute toward your education. A similar service is provided by CSS.

CFAR: Comprehensive Financial Aid Report, the formal estimate of your financial needs sent by ACT to your college or university. You can request your own copy, which explains how the evaluation was determined, by so indicating on the FFS. If you use the FAF instead, CSS will send you its assessment (called a confirmation report) automatically.

CSS: The College Scholarship Service, a part of the College Board, with home offices in Princeton, New Jersey. The CSS need analysis statement is called the FAF.

CWS: College Work-Study Program, which provides jobs for students as part of their financial aid package. All CWS jobs pay at least minimum wage and some pay more.

FAF: The Financial Aid Form, utilized by CSS to obtain information about your family finances in order to evaluate your need for other kinds of support.

FC: Family contribution—the amount determined by financial aid officials that you and your family should reasonably be expected to pay toward your education's cost.

FFS: The Family Financial Statement, utilized by ACT, is comparable to the FAF, used by CSS. Both documents are used to help measure a student's actual need for financial aid.

HPSL: The Health Professions Student Loan Program, which offers long-term loans at favorable rates for full-time students majoring in medicine or pharmacy.

I-9: The Employment Eligibility Verification form, which proves your identity and establishes that you can be legally employed. You will normally have to complete this form before you can participate in the College Work-Study Program.

IVF: Institutional Verification Form, sent to some students to obtain additional information and to document figures provided on the Family Financial Statement. (Note well: Also in the realm of verification, don't be surprised if the college or university financial aid office requests a copy of your parents' most recent federal income tax return. This is a routine procedure to make certain your family income level is as claimed. Don't take such a request personally and be offended by it; enough colleges and universities have been hoodwinked by previous financial aid requests to be convinced that some careful checking is in order.)

NSL: Nursing Student Loan program, under which students majoring in nursing can qualify for low-interest loans with excellent repayment conditions attached.

Pell Grant: Made by the federal government, and named in honor of Senator Claiborne Pell of Rhode Island, these grants go to undergraduates who can demonstrate financial need (as measured in the SAI, below).

Perkins Loan: Previously known as National Direct Student Loans, Perkins Loans are awarded through your college's financial aid office. These low-interest (5 percent) loans are named after the late Congressman Carl D. Perkins, a long-term advocate of higher education opportunities for young people.

Continued

PLUS: Short-term loans to parents to assist them in paying for the education of their children. The terms are less favorable than student loans, most of which need not be repaid until after graduation and which typically carry lower interest charges.

SAI: Student Aid Index. This is the figure, developed after analysis of your family financial situation, that determines whether you are eligible for a Pell Grant.

SAR: Student Aid Report, sent to students who have applied for Pell Grants, explaining eligibility.

SEOG: Supplemental Educational Opportunity Grant. Individual grants under the SEOG program vary, depending on other types of aid you may be getting and the availability of funds at your college.

SLS: Supplemental Loans for Students, short-term loans at up to 12 percent interest made through lenders outside the institution. The SLS name is new; previously this program bore the unfortunate title of Auxiliary Loans to Assist Students, or ALAS.

Stafford Student Loan: A Stafford Student Loan is a low-interest loan made by a private agency (a credit union, bank, savings and loan association) and insured by an agency of your state government. The federal government is committed to reinsure the loan, if necessary.

TLP: Teacher Loan Program, offered by some states to undergraduates (during their first two years of study) who aspire to careers in teaching. Those who do go on to earn teacher certification can obtain cancellation of the outstanding loan balance at the rate of 20 percent for each full year of teaching.

There are any number of other abbreviations that may be of import to individuals in given states. Students in Pennsylvania, for example, will find it useful to know about PHEAA, the Pennsylvania Higher Education Assistance Authority, the state agency that coordinates student financial aid. There are many others.

 How much money should my parents and I reasonably be expected to pay toward my college costs?

A This is one of the touchier issues in all of higher education. Many parents believe—perhaps with some justification—that colleges and universities have become overpriced, and the middle class, they are convinced, has been hit especially hard. The poorest of students can get vast amounts of financial aid, while the richest simply don't have to concern themselves with college costs much one way or the other, and everyone else gets soaked.

Estimates of each expected family contribution, carefully developed by ACT and the College Scholarship Service, are just that—estimates—and no college or university is bound by their findings. Some institutions, those with strong endowments, can subsidize students to a considerable degree. In a great many cases, and especially at private institutions, the tuition figure reported in the college catalog is much like the sticker price on a new car—shockingly high, but often subject to negotiation. (The tuition won't be cut, but the institution may increase the amount of financial aid necessary for you to meet it. The brightest students and the students from the poorest families are in the strongest negotiating positions.) The family's share of your college costs, in other words, may depend on which college you select.

As an example, consider the figures below. They represent a review of all financial aid applicants for the 1986–87 academic year at one large state university. The typical financial aid applicant at this university came from a family of four; the family's annual income was $30,222 and the family's total assets (equity in a home, investments, property, and so on) average $36,854. For each financial aid applicant, then, this university defined the family's expected share of the educational costs this way:

Family Income Range	*Average Family Portion of Costs Expected*
$0–$14,999	$1333
$15,000–$20,999	$1801
$21,000–$29,999	$2796
$30,000–$40,999	$4983
$41,000 and over	$6367

Not included here is the individual student's own expected yearly contribution of $1000 (from a part-time job, summer work, whatever). Again, these are averages. Your college may expect less—or far more.

 What other types of scholarships are there?

A There are many organizationally funded scholarships. Your parents' companies or labor unions may well have money set aside to assist employees and their dependents with higher education expenses. Foundations, religious organizations, local clubs, and civic groups often establish scholarship funds to assist individuals from specific communities or with unusual needs. Check carefully throughout your entire home community. Civic and professional clubs and local merchants frequently donate scholarship money for hometown students. Your guidance counselor or high school principal can help you identify these prospects.

Thousands of "at large" scholarships each year are awarded to individuals who can then use the money at whatever college or university they choose. There is the Ruggles Scholarship, for instance, which is presented to the student who writes the best essay on the subject of compulsory unionism; the winner gets $2000 to apply toward expenses at the college of his or her choice. The Harry S Truman Scholarships, worth thousands each, go to outstanding students who plan to pursue a career in government service. There are many others.

Because these are national in scope and not administered through any one college or university, you'll find it harder to get application forms, information about procedures, and so on. Still, if you have the drive and the patience, these scholarships could be well worth pursuing. Begin with the bulletin boards in academic departments or in the school guidance office; national and regional scholarship competitions are often posted there. Next, check with the reference department of your local library; certain publications often list national awards. You might also consult campus research offices. Normally set up as a clearinghouse for faculty research grant proposals, a well-run research office will have a useful reference library. Such directories as the *Annual Register of Grant Support* contain valuable information for students as well as faculty members.

There are, of course, several professional scholarship services available. For a fee, these companies will take an inventory of your background, conduct computer searches, and then report the possibilities that appear open to you. While some of these services are no doubt valuable, it's been said that they largely turn up information you could find out for yourself with some intelligent digging. Try a book, such as *Peterson's College Money Handbook,* first, before spending a lot of money.

Q If I transfer to another school, can I take my financial aid package with me?

A Not automatically—and perhaps not at all. Your new school may not have the scholarship/grant/loan/work-study funds available, and you may not be eligible even if it does. In any case, you will need to check in with the new institution's financial aid office to see what types of aid are available to you, present a copy of your Financial Aid Transcript (a record of the student aid you've received already; your old school can provide you with this form) and reapply.

If you are receiving scholarship support from a foundation or corporation awarded directly to you and not administered through the institution—you may well be able to move those funds with you. But you should keep the sponsoring agency fully informed.

Q Can I get a scholarship in my sophomore year if I didn't get one freshman year?

A Yes. The scholarships to incoming freshmen are awarded for academic promise, such as might be reflected in SAT or ACT scores. But after the freshman year, thousands of scholarships are given to reward performance, the work you've done since you arrived on campus. Earn an impressive GPA of about 3.5 or better, and there's a good chance you'll be considered for a portion of whatever general scholarship money your school distributes. Other scholarships may take into account campus leadership as well as academic achievement. And many departmental scholarships are reserved for upperclass students who prove themselves unusually well suited for a particular area of study. These departmental scholarships carry prestige as well as dollar value insofar as they single you out as a top prospect in your chosen career field. So don't give up if you didn't win scholarship honors going in; as the song says, it's not where you start, it's where you finish.

Q What are my chances of getting a band scholarship? Do band members have to be music majors? How much time will being in the band take?

A My knee-jerk reaction is to advise you, if you're any kind of musician at all, to get into the college band. That's the surest way I know for you to get decent seats at the football and basketball games. There are of course worthier reasons. Band members seem to enjoy themselves; they perform exciting music with fine musicians, and they participate in many on-campus events.

You aren't required to be a music major to join most university bands or even to qualify for a band scholarship. Not everybody in the college or university band is a virtuoso. Indeed, band directors welcome hard-working, enthusiastic student musicians regardless of their academic major.

Many band members at state-supported colleges and universities receive band scholarships. (By and large, scholarships at private institutions are based on financial need and not on participation in such activities as band.) However, band scholarships are usually limited to partial or full tuition support; though in some cases they may cover out-of-state fees, they don't often pay for room and board, books, or other college expenses.

Interested in applying? Contact the director of bands at the college you expect to attend and ask about an audition. At a typical audition you'll be required to play some scales and one or more prepared pieces and perhaps to do some sightreading. Some band directors may accept a taped audition, but they usually want to meet with you in person. Most auditions are scheduled in the early spring. Your high school band director can help you prepare.

How much time will the college band require? During the actual school year itself, probably less time than you spent with your high school band. The big push comes before classes begin, at a weeklong band camp where you'll learn many of the marching routines to be used throughout the football season. Band camp is grueling, sometimes involving 12 hours or more of rehearsals a day, but incoming freshmen actually find the experience an agreeable one. And by the time school starts they've already made some friends and have gained a feel for the campus. During the football season, band members generally rehearse only about an hour each weekday afternoon, and probably 2 or 3 hours on Saturday morning before a home-game performance.

It's frequently possible to earn some academic credit (though not a great deal) for band participation, and there are almost always a few travel opportunities as well. But the truly rewarding part for most band members is the fellowship. In an article in *The School Musician,* John M. Briggs had this to say about his years in the band at the University of Texas at Arlington:

> Almost nowhere can one find the closeness and unity which is so evident within the ranks and files of a university band. For as diverse in other ways as they may be, band students have in common at least a love of music—a love which, aided by the time and energy spent in rehearsal and performance, endears them to one another and to their institution.

It would indeed be difficult to find a group of students more loyal to each other or to their school. For to them, the band represents the school and is a focal point of school-related social activities. Membership in the band, then, gives to the student's college career a meaning he might miss by merely attending classes day after day. It provides him with an active role in college life rather than the passive one chosen by so many others.

Q What if my family's financial situation changes during the year?

A You should contact your school's financial aid director and provide him or her with a prompt, updated reassessment of your family's ability to help pay for your college work. There used to be a nationally agreed upon form for reporting this kind of change; the form isn't used any longer, but individual adjustments still can be made. Very often a change in family circumstances, such as a divorce or the loss of a job, will alter your level of need. So provide your school the information necessary to review and, if warranted, revise your financial aid package immediately, without your having to wait for a new academic year to begin.

Q What if I need emergency money for food or rent?

Nearly every college and university reserves a number of revolving loan funds for helping truly deserving students through crises. These loans typically run to a maximum of sixty days and must be repaid at that time. Little or no interest is charged. These loans normally cannot be used to pay tuition.

The financial aid office administers most of these funds, though the dean of your college may have access to short-term loan money that was donated to assist students in a specific field of study. One word of caution: Don't wait until the last minute to apply, because it may take four or five days to process your loan request.

Q Is ROTC a good option for me? Why or why not?

A The Reserve Officers' Training Corps (ROTC) permits students to combine military training—for which they are paid—with their academic studies. Upon graduation from college, those who have completed ROTC programs will become commissioned officers and serve a specified time on active or reserve duty. These tours of duty range from six months to four years, depending on the component (Active or Reserve) selected.

The ROTC program is a good deal for the military in that it produces many more well-educated young officers, at a much lower cost each, than the service academies (West Point, Annapolis, and the Coast Guard and Air Force academies) can. ROTC can also be a good deal for the student. The scholarships provide funding for tuition, fees, textbooks, and supplies as well as a tax-free subsistence allowance of up to $1000 each school year. Add on the pay for summer training, and an ROTC scholarship is worth literally thousands of dollars. The leadership experience is valuable, too, especially for students who one day aspire to careers in business and industry.

A most astonishing development in the military is the dramatic increase in pay and allowances. The 1988 starting pay for second lieutenants was well over $22,000. Within four years, the young officer is likely to be promoted to captain and draw about $35,000 a year. (That's the rate for single officers; those with dependents are paid more.) This is attractive compensation, thoroughly deserved, and it should go a long way toward assuring continued high quality in the country's officer corps.

For these and other reasons, ROTC enrollment is up and its image is better now, both with the general public and, significantly, with the military itself. At one time, officers commissioned through ROTC were often regarded as mere dilettantes, grossly inferior to the razor-sharp graduates of the service academies. West Pointers got more attention and better duty assignments. This caste system doesn't seem quite as evident today. ROTC-trained officers are rising rapidly through the ranks. They now comprise a substantial percentage of the top generals and admirals, and all the branches of the military seem to now have a greater respect for the richness and diversity of civilian education. Today's ROTC cadets, in other words, won't be considered second-rate officers.

The various options in the ROTC program are far more numerous and complex than can be described here. Even if your college or university doesn't have an ROTC unit, you might be able to cross-register at a school that does. For example, the University of Idaho does not have its own Air Force ROTC detachment, but students at the University of Idaho can participate in the AFROTC program at nearby Washington State University. Hundreds of such arrangements exist all over the country.

None of this should be construed as a recruiting pitch for ROTC. It isn't. There are some disadvantages to the program, not the least of which is the active or inactive duty obligation you'll face after graduation. Also, during your college years you'll have to sign up for a number of courses in military science, naval science, or aerospace studies, depending on your branch of service. This additional course work probably won't prolong your degree program, but it will cut back sharply on the number of elective subjects you can take.

Your summer vacations won't be entirely your own, either. Army ROTC cadets undergo Advanced Camp for six weeks following their junior year, and that experience is no picnic. Air Force summer field training is comparable. Naval ROTC scholarship students must complete three summer exercises, four to six weeks each; two involve training at sea, while the third is a whirlwind orientation to aviation, submarines, surface warfare, and amphibious operations with the Marine Corps. All branches expect their students to be competitive, hardworking, and capable of handling demanding physical as well as intellectual training. ROTC, in short, isn't for everybody and may not be for you.

On the other hand, there is much to be said for a program that opens up educational opportunities the way this one does, and you might want to consider it carefully.

Q. Who can I see about getting a part-time job?

A. The typical college student of today has a part-time job, and many have more than one. I'm continually impressed with—and worried about—the backbreaking job demands of some students I know. In a few cases, I don't see where there's time for study or sleep, much less for recreation. Some of those long-winded politicians and preachers who are so fond of criticizing "fun-loving students" ought to be required to work half as hard!

If you qualify for College Work-Study, you'll be offered a part-time job as part of your financial aid package. The number of hours you can put in will depend on the limits set by the admissions office. The average is about 10 hours a week.

Other, non–Work-Study part-time jobs may be listed with the dean of students or, on larger campuses, with the student employment office. Your local newspaper's classified ad pages will list many other job opportunities. College communities are geared to handle a lot of part-time help, so students who truly want jobs can almost certainly find them. The pay may run less than for comparable work elsewhere—employers in college towns enjoy an abnormally large labor pool from which to choose—but you should be able to earn enough to pay a fair-sized portion of your expenses without shattering your grades in the process.

Q What is co-op education? Would it delay my graduation? What kinds of co-op opportunities are available?

A At more than a thousand U.S. colleges and universities there is in place a somewhat more formalized and systematic plan for part-time employment called cooperative education. Under this plan, on some campuses referred to as the Earn/Learn Program, the institution arranges in advance for a number of work positions, helps place qualified students in these jobs, then monitors the work of the college students throughout the semester or the year.

For the student, co-op can lead to a nice career move later while serving as an immediate financial lifesaver. The program virtually guarantees those in it a work experience in an area related to their major. The pay is typically better than is available in most part-time jobs. (In 1988, at the University of South Carolina, for example, humanities and social sciences students average about $5 per hour on co-op jobs, while those in engineering and computer science majors were earning an average of $13 per hour.) The co-op program seems to work well for the various employers, too, in that they don't need to spend so much money recruiting. They can always arrange to get bright, able people on board (even on a seasonal basis), and, significantly, they can spot new talent for long-term commitments later. Co-op seems to benefit the institution, too, in that it makes the participating students more easily marketable after graduation.

This is not a new program; co-op arrangements were made as early as 1906. An engineering professor at Cincinnati, Herman Schneider, realized that his students were well grounded in theory but lacked practical experience. He persuaded various companies to employ his students for a time. When they returned to the classroom, he found, they brought back additional maturity and real-world expertise with them. Since then, more than 300,000 students have been placed in co-op jobs, and their earnings have made co-op education a billion-dollar industry.

Individual co-op arrangements vary. Some employers prefer to employ students for three consecutive semesters, 15 to 20 hours a week. At this rate, a student can take a normal class load. Other co-op jobs may dictate that you take off for a semester or so and work a normal 40-hour week. Does this delay graduation? Probably not, co-op executives on campus say, on the theory that an estimated 55 percent of today's students are on a five-year plan anyway. (This argument may or may not be persuasive, depending on your personal situation.)

There are opportunities for travel. The General Accounting Office, for example, regularly dispatches its co-op students to Florida, Chicago, and New York from central headquarters in Washington. The FBI, CIA, and other government agencies, as well as literally thousands of companies and nonprofit organizations, utilize college students on a co-op basis. If you are selected for an out-of-town co-op job, your campus coordinator probably will help with housing and transportation arrangements for you. There is another advantage to co-op programs, an important one: About 40 percent of all co-op students ultimately are hired by their employers for full-time jobs after graduation. On some campuses, the figure runs as high as 80 percent.

Q How many hours a week can I work without ruining my GPA?

A Some students don't have much choice. Those who are entirely self-supporting may need to put in at least a 40-hour week on the job just to make ends meet. When you're trying to pass tough courses at the same time, that kind of load can get brutal. It's generally better, I think, to cut back on the work hours and, if necessary, take out a student loan that you don't have to pay back until after you've graduated. My own theory, and this is supported by financial aid officers, is that any student whose part-time job consumes more than 20 hours a week is stretched mighty thin and quite possibly headed for emotional or academic difficulties.

On the other hand, there is now some rather interesting evidence to suggest that students on College Work-Study actually *improve* their grades, if only slightly, *as a result of their jobs.* The reason seems to be that Work-Study jobs, which typically involve clerking, filing, and photocopying (entry-level, part-time office work) around an academic department, apparently engage the student more closely with the faculty and staff (and gossip) of the institution. The student becomes far more interested in the place, develops some moxie about dealing with it, and grades improve accordingly.

Many students don't consider the College Work-Study program; they prefer jobs that are more career related. (A finance major who's looking for part-time work is likely to apply at a bank or a brokerage firm, for example.) But qualified students who do choose Work-Study may pick up a nice academic fringe benefit in addition to a regular paycheck.

How do I make a budget?

 Those few students who live like campus royalty Monday through Friday and then jet off to Acapulco or Aspen on weekends don't have to worry much about managing money. Others are so desperately poor they don't have enough money to manage. Most students, however, fall somewhere in between; they can make it—just—if they spend carefully and with restraint.

Managing money is not only a survival skill but can be an immense source of satisfaction as well. Huffy old Calvin Coolidge's pontification comes to mind: "There is no dignity quite so impressive, and no independence quite so important, as living within your means."

The first thing you have to do is to gather some factual information. Determine exactly how much operating money you have. Next, figure out how much of that income you are going to spend and for what.

If your income exceeds your anticipated expense, you don't have a problem. But if you're likely to have more going out than coming in, then something has to give. You must find ways to take in more or spend less. If there's no chance of bringing in additional income, you will need to make some decisions about allocating the resources you do have. In other words, you need to make a budget. (The term itself comes from the French "bougette," which means bag or wallet.) A budget is basically a plan that helps you to systematically use what you have to your best advantage; it also helps to ensure that your money will last until the end of the year. In and of itself, a budget won't save you money; it will, however, let you know when and if you're heading for trouble. It will also give you the solid data you need for control.

The first thing you have to do is add up your resources:

Income

    From parents   _____

    Job   _____

Income (continued)

Scholarship   _____

Student loans   _____

Savings   _____

Miscellaneous   _____

     TOTAL   _____

So much for income. Now figure out how much of that money you are going to spend:

Expenses

Tuition   _____

Housing (and utilities, if not included)   _____

Food

     Meal card   _____

     Extra meals not taken in dining hall   _____

     Snacks   _____

Transportation   _____

Car insurance   _____

Clothing   _____

Medical care (health fee, medicine, other health-related expenses)   _____

Entertainment (include Greek dues and assessments, if applicable)   _____

Books and supplies   _____

Fees (lab fees, late registration fees, private lessons, etc.)   _____

Phone calls   _____

Personal expenses (toothpaste, laundry, room furnishings, etc.)   _____

Miscellaneous   _____

     TOTAL   _____

Your totals for income and expenses should be the same. If expenses are higher than income, you'll have to adjust your estimates in various categories accordingly. Once you've done that, you've made your budget.

The next step is to actually use your budget to monitor your spending. After you've been in school for a month, examine your first batch of canceled checks to see how well you're doing. Suppose you've budgeted $250 for textbooks; you've already bought your first-semester books and spent only $85. This suggests you have a little give in this budget item; you should be able to buy more books second semester or go slightly over budget in another category this semester. But then you notice your long-distance phone bill: You've budgeted $100 for the entire year, but you've spent $24 during the first month alone. You'd better cut way back on the phone calls or shift funds away from some other item in your budget. In any event, your budget has sounded the alarm while you still have time to react.

Keep things in perspective. Don't hesitate to revise your budget as necessary, and make it flexible enough so you don't feel guilty if you don't stick to it down to the last dime. In other words, use it as a means and not as an end in itself.

The real secret to money management, of course, is to avoid unnecessary spending. Here are some modest suggestions along that line:

- Stay out of stores. What you don't see can't tempt you. If you do get dragged along by a friend, ask yourself, "Can I live without this?" That funky T-shirt you're admiring: How much would it be worth, several washings later, in your mom's garage sale? (Picture it in the 25¢-each stack.) Make a list and don't deviate from it once you get into the shop—no matter how hard the impulse-buying bug bites. (If you *really* needed it, it would be on your list, right?)

- Count yourself out when your dormmates order pizza. Say—truthfully—that you don't need the extra calories. Reach into your private stock of granola bars and let your friends envy your willpower while you save $5 for your share of the pizza.

- Don't reach out and touch someone via long distance unless you can reverse the charges. Sure you miss your friend from high school, but letters are cheaper.

- Finally, write as few checks as possible. Some stores charge as much as 50¢ to cash a check, and your bank may take 25¢ more for processing it. This means a $2.50 check can cost you as much as $3.25. Even though you don't want to carry a lot of cash around with you, be sure you have enough on hand to take care of small expenses without incurring the finance charges levied on your personal checks. Finance charges, the hidden costs you rarely anticipate, have crippled many a budget.

Q What records should I keep?

A Keep everything: fee receipts, canceled checks, housing contracts, sales slips (especially from the bookstore), grade reports, schedule cards, everything that looks official. You don't need an elaborate filing system, just a shoebox labeled Important Business; it won't take up much room and could save you a world of grief.

You should even keep a copy of the college catalog from your freshman year. The catalog is, in a way, a contract between the institution and you, and if the college changes its rules or graduation requirements, you will normally have the option (it's called a grandfather clause) of holding only to those requirements that were in force at the time you enrolled.

It's also a very good idea to hold on to all the tests and corrected papers you get back from your professors. If you have a problem with a course, or if you want to appeal a final grade, these earlier papers will be essential evidence. And your class notebooks, wretched as they may seem to you now, might well be useful at some point in your future.

CHAPTER 7

MAKING PLANS FOR THE LONG HAUL

You'll hear more homilies in an athletic team's dressing room than in a fundamentalist seminary. In my own scholastic days (and I doubt things have changed all that much since), the typical training room wall was lined with hand-lettered signs bearing assorted mottos for machos, such as WHEN THE GOING GETS TOUGH, THE TOUGH GET GOING, or A TEAM THAT WON'T BE BEAT CAN'T BE BEAT—slogans designed to raise to fever pitch the intensity of young athletes who probably possessed more intensity than ability to begin with. One of those signs, though, really hit home: WHAT YOU ARE GOING TO BE, it said, YOU ARE NOW BECOMING.

There's no way to argue with that. Your personality, your level of ambition and drive, your priorities and choices—all are beginning to form a pattern. Though certainly not irreversible at this point, a trend is in fact being established: You're moving toward where you're going to be. It's time, in other words, to begin thinking about some decisions that lie ahead. But first, a consideration of values:

Q How concerned are colleges with ethics and morality?

A Not enough. A generation ago, one of my own professors admitted during one of his lectures: "We call ourselves higher education. We do a pretty fair job of teaching people how to make a living. We don't do a very good job of teaching people how to get along together and behave in a decent and honorable way."

That was before Watergate and the latest round of insider trading scandals on Wall Street, before the word "sleaze" became an all-too-familiar part of the national vocabulary.

America's earliest institutions of higher learning were regarded by settlers primarily as a means of training ministers and devout laymen in the faith. Soon after that, political leaders realized that more people than ministers needed advanced education; the state-supported colleges and universities represent one response to the problem. Even in the state schools, though, many professors saw their role as that of keeper of social traditions and values. Lectures reflected a stern moral tone; outside the classroom, student behavior was closely monitored (colleges acted *in loco parentis*—in place of parents), and disciplinary codes were tough.

More recently, however, and especially since the sixties, students have demanded—and gotten—far more freedom outside the classroom. More to the point, professors redefined their role; most of us feel our job is to inform our students, not preach to them or attempt to prescribe their moral behavior. The pendulum, in short, has swung back the other way—perhaps too far. Consider:

- the conflict of interest charges facing high government officials
- the bribery, corruption, and illegal trading activities that have rocked the financial world
- Medicare kickbacks, unnecessary surgical procedures and other embarrassments to the medical establishment
- the shady arms deals that led to shakeups within the military and intelligence establishments

And so on—and on. These offenses were not committed by underprivileged high school dropouts; they represent the work of some highly educated individuals who achieved technical brilliance while managing, at the same time, to lose their moral compass.

The academic community's response, slow in coming, has been to create and emphasize courses in ethical behavior. Usually offered in specific disciplines (schools of business, law, medicine, education, and mass communications), these classes explore means of setting standards of behavior in the workplace as well as provide students a methodology for developing moral judgments about current professional dilemmas. Facing the medical field, for example, there are profoundly important questions connected with prolonging life and, through genetic engineering, shaping—and even creating—life. Business and political science students can learn ways to combine material success with social consciousness. Mass communications students analyze a whole range of gritty ethical dilemmas, including freebies, junkets, shielding the confidentiality of news sources, unwarranted invasions of personal privacy, and avoiding bias in reporting the news.

Throughout academia there has evolved no consensus as to how ethical behavior should be taught. Most ethics courses, the ones I know about, anyway, are designed to confront students with a whole barrage of ethical dilemmas, then require the student to think through his or her own solution to each. Much outside reading and research are expected. A well-taught ethics class is tough, but if it helps the student develop a personal and professional philosophy reflecting worthy values and ethical standards, the experience can be invaluable. Complexities and uncertainties loom large in the years ahead; increasingly, success will be, or should be, measured not only by what you will achieve, but how you did it.

 When should I choose my major?

A A major, or field of concentration, as it's sometimes called, is simply a series of courses designed to provide you with a strong background in the academic area you're most attracted to. No more, no less. Most of the time, declaring a major is a simple process. All you have to do is write in your choice on your registration form, and the administration takes it from there. This declaration is usually less urgent than most students or parents think it is ("I'd feel so much better about sending Alvin to college if only he knew *exactly* what he wanted to study. . . .").

Faculty advisers have managed to learn a thing or two about majors. First, a student probably will devote only one fourth to one third of his or her total course work to the major field anyway; most undergraduate hours will be consumed by general requirements and elective subjects. A major is thus only one part of a college education. Another historical truth is that students are eminently likely to change their major (see p. 150) once it's been declared. This often alarms parents, but it shouldn't; after all, college is a time of growth and exposure to new subjects and different ideas. A change in the major, particularly during the student's first two years, probably won't impede normal progress toward graduation.

In some career fields, the student's undergraduate major may not matter. Law is one of these. Most law school admission policies recognize that a background in almost any field of study can be valuable. Advertising is another case in point. Highly successful advertising people are known to have majored in business, where they learned marketing; in journalism, where they got some understanding of the mass media; in English, where they studied great writing; in fine arts, where they were exposed to creative concepts; or in psychology, where they learned behavior patterns.

For other lines of work, however, the undergraduate major is the direct, and possibly the only, route that leads you into your chosen field. If you want to be a grade-school teacher, the sooner you declare a major in elementary education, the better. Fulfilling rigid teacher certification requirements will take up most of your course schedule, and a late decision could delay your degree by a year or so. Engineering students also face a tough, complex set of requirements, as do students in music and a number of other areas.

By and large, though, you do have some room for maneuvering, so before you declare a major you might consider the following:

- Don't panic if you're unsure. Even if the academic bureaucrats are hovering over you for a decision (don't blame them; they're simply trying to shuttle your records over to the right department and assign you to an appropriate faculty adviser), you can usually fend them off for a while by declaring yourself "undecided." Basic course requirements for the freshman and sophomore years are fairly standard anyway. Keep chipping away at your required courses so that when you do make up your mind you'll have clear sailing inside your major field.

- Remember that academic counselors and aptitude testing agencies are available to you on campus to help you clarify your thinking about a career choice. If you decide on a vocational goal, the problem of choosing a major usually takes care of itself.
- Be wary of choosing a trendy major that may not amount to much or be marketable after graduation. In recent years, colleges have contrived a number of fun-sounding majors—American studies, women's studies, ethnic studies, environmental studies, and the like—that might not open as many employment opportunities for you as more traditional majors.
- On the other hand, it might be possible—and in some cases highly desirable—for you to design your own major. You choose a theme and then develop it with courses from a number of departments. Let's say, for example, that you're interested in becoming an expert on Latin America; you could probably gain approval to develop an interdisciplinary major in that important area. The courses for your major, in this case, would be drawn from such departments as political science, history, economics, foreign languages, sociology, and geography. Individualized majors generally involve additional course work and endorsements from a faculty adviser and a dean. Choosing an individualized major can be a sign of intellectual creativity and curiosity, determination, assertiveness, industriousness, and other characteristics potential employers look for.
- Think beyond the entry-level job and be careful not to limit your options. If your dream is to be a television sportscaster, you'd do well to develop a course of study that also includes TV programming, management, accounting, communications law, and broadcast production. Twenty years from now you may be running the station.

Q Suppose my plans change in a year or two. How difficult is it to change my major?

A From the college administration's point of view, a change of majors is a simple, routine bookkeeping transaction. All you'll probably need to do is (1) notify the department in which your records are currently kept that you're making the change and request that your records be forwarded to the new department, (2) ask the secretary of the new department to assign you a faculty adviser, and (3) indicate your new major on the enrollment form the next time you register.

There could be a problem in gaining admission to the new department. Suppose, for example, you want to switch your major from English in the College of Arts and Sciences to marketing in the College of Business Administration. But Business, faced with too many majors, has adopted a policy that all entering transfers must have at least a 2.5 GPA, while yours is only a 2.3. You might ask for a waiver and try to get in anyway, but unless your petition is approved, you simply won't be able to become a marketing major. A number of high-demand departments have tightened admissions standards, so you'd better do some checking before you make a final decision.

If you're otherwise qualified, however, you'll find that changing your major is a relatively quick and painless procedure. This doesn't mean it should be done capriciously. While trying to decide whether to change your major, you might discover that the new department has an entirely different set of requirements—additional courses that could keep you in college for another year or more. For this reason alone, then, it's a good idea to hold off declaring a new major until you're reasonably sure of your commitment to it. While you're making up your mind, you can list yourself as "undecided." This way you'll still get a faculty adviser (one who has a broad understanding of just this kind of problem), and you can profitably spend your time whacking away at general distribution requirements.

 ## Where can I get help in choosing a career?

Your college or university, acutely aware that its reputation is directly linked to the career successes of its graduates, most likely operates a placement office that is open to everyone connected with the institution, from freshmen to alumni. You can find a wealth of information here on job-hunting techniques, individual companies, graduate study, summer and short-term employment, and career opportunities in general. In addition to supplying reading material, placement office counselors often hold seminars and clinics on interviewing techniques, career planning, and related vocational topics.

Most undergraduates fail to make full use of campus placement services. "My biggest problem," a placement director once told me, "is that students wait until they're seniors to come see us."

I don't believe it's wise to spend your college years in an obsessive, single-minded quest for a job—your educational concerns should be far broader than this—but I do believe it's a mistake to ignore your career plans entirely.

I've seen too many tearful graduating seniors who put off thinking about life after college until the last weeks of the last semester.

So check in with your placement office early; find out about what kinds of specific advice you can count on later. You may also do some preliminary reading about various types of vocations so you can start to narrow your range of career choices.

If you're completely at sea about the types of work for which you may be suited, pay a visit to the counseling office. Your first interview here should provide a trained psychologist with a good idea of your background and interests. Afterward you may be encouraged to take a battery of aptitude tests that can be used in follow-up sessions as you begin to define your vocational goals. There may be a charge for processing the tests; the counseling itself is normally provided free of charge. The tests will suggest several occupational areas for which you appear to be suited, and, conversely, point out other career fields that you probably wouldn't really like. Testing won't reveal any magic, surefire career formula for you to follow, but it can provide information that can be enormously helpful to you. Most of all, you'll actually be *doing* something about planning your career, instead of just waiting around passively in hopes that lightning will strike.

Q What is the best way to cope with anxiety about career goals?

A Many people seem to know, almost from birth, *exactly* what it is they want to do with their lives. These fortunate, sometimes infuriating, individuals can spend their college years in efficient, untroubled preparation for their careers. If you happen to associate with such students, you may be intimidated by them or you may consider yourself a failure if you, too, don't have your life all planned out by the end of freshman year.

Here, again, you'd do well to visit the counseling office. It could be that you simply don't yet know enough about yourself or about specific careers to begin working toward a solution. A case in point: Bryan was floundering through his undergraduate years, unhappy with his major in business but, at the same time, afraid to try something else. After several months of frustration, during which time he became increasingly unhappy with himself, he went to the counseling office to have a talk and take a battery of vocational tests. The tests suggested that Bryan appeared well suited for a number of career fields, one of them being cartography. Bryan's first response was relief: "Gee, I must have more aptitude than I thought." His next: "What does a cartographer do?" (Makes maps.) Then: "How do I find out more about this type of work?" His research led him to a major in geography and, after graduation (with grades much improved), to a promising job with a publisher specializing in maps and related reference works. Not every visit to the counseling office produces such cheerful results, but many do. Bryan's story, which is true, is by no means an isolated example.

Q What if I want to take a year off?

A Our system is programmed to move young men and women directly out of high school into jobs or college. Those who do go on to college have about four extra years in which to decide on the careers they wish to follow, and to prepare themselves accordingly. Then, following the commencement ceremony, they should glide smoothly into their chosen businesses or professions.

You may not fit this mold. If not, then you might want to withdraw for a time and break the rhythm in order to travel, to rethink your goals and priorities, to gain a new sense of perspective—in other words, to "stop out." Stopping out—as opposed to quitting school—can be a positive, even life-changing, experience.

There are risks involved. For one thing, your parents may object and order you to move out of the house and make your own way. ("When you get back in school and know what you want to do, I'll help. But I won't support you while you're doing nothing.") Also, you may not be able to land much of a job; employers might (correctly) regard you as a transient, and, moreover, you'll be in competition for the better positions with people who already have their degree. And if you do get interesting work, you may then find it difficult to return to the campus once you've tasted independence and begun to earn your own money, thus defeating the purpose of your stop-out.

Stop-outs who do come back to school, however, are often happier, more successful students. Their work experience helps them in the classroom. (Some even obtain college credit for it through an experiential education program.) They're usually better organized, more mature, and more sure of themselves.

If you do stop out—and this is a serious step, far more serious than the relatively brief discussion of it here might indicate—make some plans beforehand. Set goals. ("During my stop-out I intend to decide on a new career objective and a new major; I want to see if I would enjoy a job in sales.") You want to do more with this time than just drift along aimlessly. Above all, keep in touch with your parents in a positive, constructive way during this period. It's natural for them to worry about you; just don't make them worry excessively or unnecessarily.

Finally, be certain to leave school on good terms. Don't blow off your grades at year's end. ("The hell with this; I'm leaving school next month anyway.") Your transcript, warts and all, will be there when you get back. Let the college authorities—the registrar, the dean, your faculty adviser—know you'll be away for a time, but that you do expect to complete your studies. Under these circumstances, it's entirely possible you'll be able to reclaim your financial aid package, among other benefits, when you return.

Q I'm very interested in spending my junior year in Europe. There are so many overseas study programs available! How can I begin to evaluate them?

A All overseas travel-study programs look good, and most of them are. The difficulty (and this is a problem most of us would love to have) comes in fitting your needs and your budget into just the right foreign-study package.

An excellent guide for analyzing overseas study programs has been prepared by Pat Kern McIntyre, formerly of the U.S. Office of Education. Her 68-page booklet, *Study and Teaching Opportunities Abroad,* is available at about $5 a copy from the Government Printing Office, Washington, D.C. 20402. And while the federal government does not get into the business of officially recognizing and evaluating foreign travel/study programs, it does suggest some sensible guidelines:

Know the sponsor. Check with previous participants. Make sure you identify the agency bearing legal responsibility. Look into the program's history. Don't hesitate to ask questions. A reputable organization will welcome your inquiries.

Check the sponsor's finances. Be sure you understand whether basic fees will cover all expenses for travel or whether there will be some add-on charges later (for taxis, buses, side trips, etc.). Will medical and accident insurance be provided in the basic fee? What provisions are made in case of cancellations?

Consider the contingency plans. Find out whether arrangements exist for students who are in difficulty. Would they be sent home? At whose expense? Would there be extra charges or penalty fees for returning early?

Investigate housing and study facilities. Knowing where you'll be living is important. In foreign countries, as here at home, there are wildly different opinions as to what constitutes adequate housing.

Compare the sponsor's objectives with your own. Some programs emphasize travel and sightseeing, others concentrate on foreign language study, while still others focus on a specific subject area, such as music, art, architecture, the mass media, or literature. Be sure your interests are compatible with the priorities of the program.

Critically review the program of study. If your objective is to study at a foreign university, find out whether you will actually work with the top people there. Will you be taught by temporary replacements or part-time staff members? To a great extent the success or failure of an overseas study program depends on the teachers, so you need to know who they would be. Also make sure you know the language of instruction and have a good idea of the academic demands that will be placed on you.

Investigate the qualifications of the staff. (This includes tour directors and counselors.) And perhaps most important of all, find out who the other students will be and how they were selected.

In addition to these evaluation criteria, *Study and Teaching Opportunities Abroad* contains a helpful listing of information sources regarding travel tips, financial assistance, work opportunities, and the like.

A trip overseas, whether it's a quickie tour or a semester or year of study at a foreign university, can be a marvelous experience and usually proves to be a most significant part of one's education. The great majority of students return from a trip overseas with their spirits lifted, their eyes opened, and their sights raised. Careful checking and advance planning can enhance the travel even more. Bon voyage!

Q **Is graduate study in the arts and sciences a good idea? How hard is it to be admitted to graduate school?**

A A graduate program, a college within a college, provides advanced, specialized instruction for students seeking master's degrees and doctorates. The graduate schools of most universities share buildings and faculty with the undergraduate school. The courses and the approach are what make graduate programs unique.

In some career fields—college teaching, for example—graduate study is essential. In others, a graduate degree may not be required, but having one can certainly improve your chances in the job market and bring you a higher starting salary.

Graduate school will require a serious commitment of your time (the better part of two years for a master's degree, four years or more for a Ph.D.), and for some this could amount to educational overkill. Depending on your career objectives, you may be better off moving immediately into the job market for some work experience instead. (Sometimes it's better, in other words, to quit warming up down in the bull pen and get into the game!)

Another decision to make is when to go to graduate school. Is it better to move straight through? Or should you get a few years of career experience under your belt first? There are cogent arguments on both sides, and you should take them into account—along with all the other considerations about personal and professional matters that go into a career decision of this magnitude.

Every professor you have is presumably an expert on the subject of graduate school, and most profs are pleased to talk with you about it as you attempt to make up your mind. Get as much information and advice as you can. The academic world is a fairly small one, and you're likely to find professors on your own campus who are familiar with practically any graduate program you are considering.

No matter where you do attend graduate school, you'll discover an environment entirely different from the one you're in now. Instead of large lecture classes, you'll be placed in small, competitive seminars. You'll be expected to work harder, and far more attention will be paid to you by the senior members of the faculty (a decidedly mixed blessing!). And, because you may receive a teaching or research assistantship (as many graduate students do), you become much more involved with the staff and the workings of your department.

Graduate school will also change your intellectual and professional outlook. During your undergraduate years you are essentially passive; knowledge is dispensed to you, and your job is, by and large, merely to understand it and store it (at least until the next test!). As a graduate student, though, you'll assume a more active role, one in which you begin to learn how to generate new knowledge. There is a strong research emphasis in most graduate degree programs.

Graduate instruction is highly personalized and therefore costly for the institution; this is one of the main reasons most graduate programs are small and selective. Graduate admissions committees will want a great deal of information about you, which means you will have to put a lot of time and effort into preparing your application.

Acceptance or rejection by a graduate school will hinge on some combination of the following: your undergraduate grades, especially those you earn in your major field in your junior and senior years; your performance on the Graduate Record Examination (GRE); recommendations from your professors and others who know your work; and the statement of purpose you submit as part of your application.

You should also be doing some careful selecting as well. Check into the quality of the program—not as it might have been when your favorite professor did graduate work there, but as it is today. Examine specific degree requirements, which will vary greatly from one place to another. (There can be literally years of difference among various universities in the length of time realistically needed to complete a graduate degree program.) Cost is always a consideration for graduate students, and so is the extent of financial support offered. In many cases, the dollar value of the graduate assistantship/ fellowship will become the deciding factor.

If you are serious about graduate study, then apply to a number of schools. (If you aren't serious, get a job instead. Graduate school is tough enough even if you love it.) Applying is a time-consuming and expensive business—the forms are lengthy and there's a processing fee for each application—but you'll need to keep open as many options as you can. Also, it's best to start as early as the fall semester of your senior year, if at all possible. (This means you'll need to do your preliminary screening and send for catalogs and application forms well before then.) Many graduate schools begin awarding fellowships and assistantships by mid-February for the next academic year. You might still get accepted into the program if you apply late, but your chances for financial support are much slimmer.

Finally, I'd recommend that you consider transferring to another school for your graduate work. Even though you may have to give up convenience and familiarity with your surroundings, there's much to be said for obtaining an additional point of view through exposure to a new environment and a different faculty.

Q How do I prepare for a professional school? What are my chances of getting in?

A What's already been said about graduate study—the changed environment, the intensity, the complex admissions process—applies as well to a large extent to schools of law, medicine, business, and theology. Even so, each profession selects and prepares its would-be entrants somewhat differently, and the differences are worth noting. Here's an overview of four types of professional schools:

LAW SCHOOL

There is no one prescribed way to prepare for law school. Almost all schools of law now require that their applicants be college graduates, but the bachelor's degree can be in virtually any field of study. Essentially, law schools are looking for students who can reason and analyze with great skill, who can think critically, who have an understanding of human institutions and values, and who are able to express themselves well. The most common prelaw majors include political science, English, history, accounting, business administration, and journalism. No matter what the major, developing writing and speaking skills is a vitally important part of the undergraduate course of study for prelaw students.

Grades are important, as is performance on the Law School Admission Test (LSAT) in determining who is accepted for the study of law. But other factors are usually considered also. For example, the *trend* of the grades is often taken into account. If a student started poorly in college but improved markedly in later years, he or she is likely to be judged more favorably than another student with the same GPA but a record of level or declining performance. Letters of recommendation can help—or hurt. The reputation of the undergraduate school the applicant attended may be taken into account; some colleges are known to demand more of their students than others. A heavy load of outside work can be a plus; admissions officers are impressed with students who have helped support themselves through college. Involvement in extracurricular activities can also be a good sign. "After all," one law school dean explained, "lawyers don't work in a vacuum. They must understand people and appreciate their problems."

What are your chances of getting into law school? That depends on where you apply. If you're only interested in one specific institution, you may have a problem. If you're flexible and willing to apply to a number of schools, however, your chances are better.

At the University of Kentucky, as an example of a state school, the law admissions staff processes about 750 applications a year. About 450 of the applicants are residents of the state. From the total of 750, 160 will be enrolled; about 90 percent of them will be Kentuckians. As is the case with many state-supported institutions, priority must be given to local applicants. Only 14 out-of-state applicants will be chosen, so obviously the in-state people have the edge. Residency quotas do not normally apply, of course, at private law schools.

On a national basis, the admissions picture is fairly promising. In a typical year, about 70,000 students apply for admission to schools of law. More than 47,000 of these are offered a place in at least one accredited law school, and about 40,000 students actually enroll. This puts the overall odds at better than 60–40 in your favor.

Once admitted, most law students stick. Returning again to the University of Kentucky, we find that officials predict that only 10 to 12 of the 160 entering students will flunk out. About half of these will be readmitted for a second chance. Three to 5 additional students will leave the law school for other reasons. The others, about 95 percent of those admitted, will be graduated with law degrees.

For more information, look for a copy of the *Prelaw Handbook,* prepared by the Law School Admission Council and the Association of American Law Schools. It's available at college bookstores or through the Law School Admission Service, P.O. Box 2000, Newtown, Pennsylvania 18940.

MEDICAL SCHOOL

Nearly every campus has a premed adviser who can help you chart your course toward medical school. There is no specific premed major, though about two thirds of the country's medical school applicants major in one of the sciences. Your undergraduate studies should nevertheless include one full year each of general chemistry, organic chemistry, biology, and physics—each with labs. Some medical schools may tack on additional requirements such as calculus, but as a general rule you're free to major in anything from agriculture to English so long as you cover those basic science courses. Some medical schools will admit you after you've finished 90 semester hours; others require a bachelor's degree.

Virtually all U.S. medical schools require or strongly recommend that you take the Medical College Admission Test (MCAT), a daylong standardized exam. It's administered twice a year and should be taken about eighteen months before you plan to enter medical school. There's no such thing as a passing MCAT grade; scores are evaluated and used differently by each school.

Undergraduate grades are terribly important; as a matter of fact, they're often regarded as the single most likely predictor of medical school performance. Med school admissions officers do, however, take into account the fact that grading policies vary widely around the country. First-year med students in the 1970s and early 1980s racked up a national GPA of 3.5 as undergraduates. Some students with lower GPAs were admitted, in most cases, because they showed personal and professional traits, such as steady improvement in academic performance toward the end of their undergraduate years or a high MCAT score. The personal interview could also make or break a medical school applicant, although if academic and/or MCAT performance isn't convincing, applicants usually don't make it to the interview stage. During the interview, the committee will be looking for evidence of such things as social and intellectual maturity, leadership, drive, initiative, common sense, and—perhaps most of all—whether you know what you're letting yourself in for by seeking a career in medicine. (A question frequently asked is "Can you imagine what it's like spending the rest of your life around people who are sick?")

A good premed adviser will urge you from your freshman year on to challenge the desire you think you have to practice medicine. Spend time at a clinic or hospital, and while you're there get as involved as you can in the treatment of patients. You may well decide that med school isn't for you after all.

More than 35,000 men and women a year currently apply for medical school, and about half of them are accepted (though not all of these, by any means, by their first-choice school). If you're aiming for a state-supported medical school, apply first to the schools in your home state; your chances at an out-of-state public medical school are truly slim. Private medical schools, of course, can and do accept qualified applicants from across the country.

If you want more information, including detailed descriptions of programs at every accredited medical school in the United States, ask your premed adviser or your reference librarian for the latest edition of *Medical School Admission Requirements.* You can also order a copy for $10 from the Association of American Medical Colleges, One Dupont Circle, NW, Washington, D.C. 20036.

BUSINESS SCHOOL

In 1965, some 5,000 persons were graduated with a Master of Business Administration (M.B.A.) degree; by 1982, the yearly M.B.A. output had shot up to 57,000. More than 600 colleges and universities now offer the degree, and the number is increasing at the rate of about thirty-five new schools each year as more and more young people choose the M.B.A. as the first step in what they hope will be a challenging and prosperous career in management.

A typical M.B.A. curriculum calls for at least one full year of tough, competitive graduate work in such subjects as organizational behavior, managerial economics, financial/managerial accounting, marketing management, legal and regulatory environment, business conditions analysis, production management, and quantitative business analysis.

If you're thinking of going on for an M.B.A., you should prepare by taking a full year of accounting and at least one semester of calculus. Some M.B.A. programs require additional undergraduate course work, but most schools may permit you to be conditionally admitted for M.B.A. study while you chip away at any undergraduate prerequisites you may have missed. It's not necessary to major in business—many liberal arts graduates are excellent M.B.A. candidates—but if you do have your bachelor's degree in business you'll probably be able to complete the M.B.A. work more rapidly.

In many schools it's possible to earn the M.B.A. degree as either a full-time or part-time student. A number of M.B.A. programs, in fact, are geared for men and women who are already in the business world. Many schools offer other degrees in business as well, such as the Doctor of Business Administration (D.B.A.) for those interested in research, teaching business at the college level, or business consulting.

Your admission to an accredited M.B.A. program will be based on such criteria as your undergraduate record, your performance on the Graduate Management Admission Test (GMAT), your accomplishments or experience at work, recommendations, and such intangibles as motivation, talent for leadership, and emotional stability and maturity.

The Graduate Management Admission Council publishes *The Official Guide to the M.B.A.,* which contains descriptions of most M.B.A. programs in the country. Your library or business school should have copies. If not, you can order one for about $10 from the GMAT Program Direction Office, Educational Testing Service, Princeton, New Jersey 08541.

THEOLOGICAL/DIVINITY SCHOOL

There are about 160 accredited seminaries in the United States, all members of the Association of Theological Schools. These schools all require that you have a bachelor's degree before beginning their programs. Ideally, your transcript should reflect a strong showing in English, history, philosophy, psychology, and sociology, as well as some aptitude for language study. Many seminaries will require you to take Greek and Hebrew; a few of them assume you are already familiar with one or both of these languages, so you'd better plan accordingly.

There are distinct differences in doctrine among theological seminaries— even among seminaries representing the same religious denomination—so you'd do well to examine a school's point of view before applying. In many cases, the faculty will have developed a comprehensive statement that explains how religious issues will be interpreted and presented. If the theological stances at one seminary disturb you, you'll want to apply elsewhere. In any case, learn ahead of time what doctrines you'll be dealing with, and how.

The primary purpose of most seminaries, of course, is to prepare men and women for the clergy. The professional degree normally granted is called the Master of Divinity, and it requires three full years of study. Not everyone who enrolls in a seminary necessarily wants or expects to become a member of the ordained clergy, however. Many students, including those who simply are interested in the study of religion, enroll in a two-year program leading to a Master of Arts. There are still other degrees and options offered around the country.

Enrollment for religious study varies with the times. During relatively quiet, prosperous years, many seminaries operate at less than capacity. Wars and depressions, however, bring on big increases in numbers of applicants. Your chances for admission, in other words, may well be connected to the current emotional state of the country.

Q How can I get credit for experiential education?

A On many campuses it's possible under certain conditions to earn academic credit for a field- or community-based learning experience that's carried out under the direction of a faculty member.

Suppose you're majoring in telecommunications, for example, and a local TV station has an opening for a part-time production assistant to help with the early evening news. The job would give you hands-on experience in your field, and it obviously has intrinsic educational value as well.

Filing for experiential education credit typically involves filling out a "learning contract"—something that specifies how many hours a week you'll be at the TV station, what duties you will perform there, the academic and professional objectives that justify taking on this work, and the ways in which your performance will be evaluated. Your faculty adviser (who will ultimately determine your grade), your job supervisor, and the dean of your college will all have to sign the contract. The amount of time you put in and your school's policies on EXP credit will determine how many hours you get.

Your college or university may have a central office that coordinates experiential education. If not, ask someone in your dean's office for a list of "internships" that might be worth college credit to you. If you can't find what you want among the standard internships, you may want to create your own experiential learning situation. Thousands of students do, and they manage to obtain credit for off-campus work done in a wide variety of fields. If you are able to articulate your learning objectives and arrange for faculty supervision, there's a good chance you can pick up some credit hours for work done outside the classroom.

Q How do I go about finding a summer job?

A The job market may not be Topic A with most students, but if it isn't A, it's at least B or C. Professors share your concern. Far from being aloof, insensitive ogres, most of us honestly do care about students and are willing to help them in their job searches as best we can. The typical prof will devote a good many hours a year to counseling students on career possibilities and writing reference letters to prospective employers.

Most of the work, however, has to be done by you. Each person has something to sell—knowledge, experience, talent, skill, or time. The trick comes in packaging your assets effectively and in directing them to the employers who are most likely to be interested in buying.

Where are the jobs? One school of thought suggests that the employment search, like charity, should begin at home. "Use your family, your friends, your contacts," one university placement director urged some students of mine. "Use any kind of personal or business or family or political influence you can. I know there are students who don't want to do that. They say, 'I'm not going to take advantage of my family situation. I want to prove I can make it on my own.' Sorry, but I think that's baloney. You'll have the rest of your life to prove yourself. Your family can't keep a job for you once you've got it. That part is up to you and your abilities. But if your family or friends can help you get your foot in the door, then let them."

Ask your teachers for assistance, too, especially those who do consulting work or maintain close contact with the "real world." Engineering professors, for instance, routinely guide students into permanent or summer jobs in industry, as do profs in the business school, journalism department, and so on. If you're friendly with your faculty adviser—and you certainly ought to be—explain that you're in the job market and ask for information and assistance. Even if your adviser can't help you personally, he or she may be able to direct you to a colleague who can.

Your next stop should be the placement office, a clearinghouse for news about job openings. Many companies now have summer internship programs, and the placement office staff will serve as official contacts on your campus. Lists of vacancies and interview schedules are posted frequently—virtually every day, on some campuses—so you'll need to check in at regular intervals.

Quite a few summer jobs are available in local, state, and national government, but getting information on these positions is not always easy. Some notices may be sent to the political science department, for example, while others go to the College of Agriculture, the sociology department, or some other academic units. Unless your school is large enough to have an office that specializes in government jobs, your best solution is simply to trudge around the campus making periodic inspections of departmental bulletin boards.

Still another possibility, one I'm surprised students don't use more, is the classified ad section of the newspaper. Your main library subscribes to many newspapers, probably including one published in the city where you'd most like to work. Even though you're operating at long range, and it's likely that you would be invited in for an interview, you do stand a chance of landing a job via this route.

You might also assume the initiative by writing directly to specific companies you're interested in, without waiting for notice of a vacancy to appear.

Sometimes a well-crafted letter along with a businesslike résumé will strike a responsive chord with a key executive. Even if you aren't hired for the summer, this enterprising approach might still get you an invitation to visit the office, meet some key executives, and perhaps lay the groundwork for a permanent job after graduation.

By now it should be clear that job hunting is a more or less continuous process that requires time, effort, imagination, and a variety of strategies. The experience and insights you acquire while looking for summer work will prove especially valuable to you later on, when you begin planning in earnest for the career you hope to launch when your college days are finished.

How do I write a résumé?

A résumé is a summary of your qualifications, carefully selected and presented, as a rule, in outline form. You'll want to keep the résumé as brief as possible—one or two pages should do for most young people—yet comprehensive enough to supply the specific information your prospective boss will need to make a judgment about your background. Here's one format you might wish to follow:

1. Identifying information. Your name, address (campus as well as permanent home address), and phone number. Additional personal data, such as your date of birth, a statement about the condition of your health, your marital status (optional), your hobbies, favorite pastimes, and so on, may be put at the end of the résumé.
2. Your job objective. This need not be terribly specific; just mention the type of work you hope to find, such as "sales" or "public relations." You'll certainly want to tailor your résumé to fit each specific job application. If you're applying for summer work as a lifeguard at the beach, you wouldn't want to list your ultimate job objective, which may be in nuclear physics. Your immediate objective is to land a summer job as a lifeguard, so let your résumé say so.
3. Your educational background. List the high school from which you were graduated and the college or university you're currently attending. Point out courses or subjects you've completed that pertain to your job objective. Also mention extracurricular activities (these can indicate leadership potential), honors and scholarships you have won, and so on.

Continued on p. 168

Sample Résumé

Bradley Truman
118 Columbia Terrace
Lexington, KY 40502
606-343-4455

Home address:
709 West 2nd Street
Louisville, KY 45353
502-276-1643

<u>Job objective</u>   Advertising sales

<u>Educational background</u>

Arrow Creek High School, Louisville, KY. Graduated in May 1987.
    Ranked 23rd in class of 354.
    Varsity basketball, three years. Won "110 percent" award in senior year.
    Member, Beta Club, service and leadership society.
    Member, Spanish Club.
    Advertising staff, <u>The Admiral</u>, student newspaper. Sold ads for three years. Did own layouts.

University of Kentucky, Lexington. Expected graduation: May 1991.
    Advertising staff, <u>Kentucky Kernel</u>, independent student daily newspaper. Serve approximately 25 clients. Do own layouts, develop own sales presentation. Some market research.
    Member, Kappa Sigma social fraternity. Vice president of pledge class in freshman year. Presently assistant rush chairman.
    Have completed Principles of Advertising (grade of A) and one introductory course in Marketing.

<u>Work history</u>
    August 1987–present. Advertising salesman (part-time), <u>Kentucky Kernel</u>.
    June 1987–August 1987. Pizza Hut, Russell Mall, Louisville, KY. Served three weeks as night counter supervisor.
    May 1985–June 1987. Midtowne Cinema, Louisville, KY. Worked nights and weekends while in high school as ticket taker, assistant cashier, and salesclerk in concessions.

Continued on next page

Sample Résumé *(continued)*

Miscellaneous qualifications
Familiar with VDT, ad layout, newspaper production.
Fluent in spoken and written Spanish.

Personal information
Born .... December 19, 1969
Health...................................... Excellent
Hobbies .... Jogging, golf
Marital status .... Single

References (by permission)

Prof. Mary Lou Dennis
Department of Marketing
University of Kentucky
Lexington, KY 40506

Mr. H. B. Lute
Director of Publications
University of Kentucky
Lexington, KY 40506

Mr. Clyde B. Bolden, Jr.
Manager, Pizza Hut
Russell Mall
Louisville, KY 45353

Mr. Seth Johnson
Manager, Midtowne Cinema
Midtowne Plaza
Louisville, KY 45353

Sample Letter of Application
(to accompany résumé)

Mr. Joseph A. Piscoonyak
Director of Advertising
Milwaukee <u>Times</u>
Times Plaza
Milwaukee, Wisconsin 58989

Dear Mr. Piscoonyak,

I am writing to apply for a position in your Summer Intern Program. I believe that working for the <u>Times</u> would be a valuable learning experience for me and an important step in my career. I hope one day to work as an advertising sales representative for a metropolitan newspaper.

The enclosed résumé lists my qualifications. Please note that I am currently a part-time advertising salesman for our student daily newspaper here at the University of Kentucky. In this capacity, I have developed sales presentations and serviced about twenty-five active accounts.

I believe that this experience combined with my own enthusiasm for the field would make me a useful member of your Summer Intern team, and I can assure you that I would make the most of this exciting opportunity.

Please let me know if I need to provide additional information. Thank you very much for considering me.

Sincerely,

Bradley Truman

Bradley Truman

4. Work history. Make a separate entry for each job you've had, beginning with the most recent and moving backward. Briefly mention the tasks you performed and highlight all the positive features you can; for example, you might want to include the fact that you supervised other workers or that you received a letter of commendation. Any type of work is important, by the way. Don't omit a job just because you think the work was too menial to mention. As a rule, employers look favorably on young people who have shown the initiative to find jobs of any kind.

5. Miscellaneous qualifications. Here is your opportunity to list any special skills you may have, such as knowledge of a foreign language or the ability to operate various office machines. You might also include in this section any volunteer work you may have done.

6. References. Give the names of three persons who know you and the work you have done. Teachers and former employers are good choices. Be sure to provide the addresses and titles of your references. And, as a courtesy, get the permission of the persons you plan to list.

Get the résumé typed and have plenty of copies made. Quick-print shops can do the job fairly inexpensively. (It's not a good idea to give out a photocopy; this makes it plain you gave the original to someone else.)

There is no one best way to prepare a résumé. Some employers are demons for conciseness and believe a résumé should be limited to a single page. Others prefer more information, a fuller account of your background and credentials. For more ideas and samples of different types of résumés, consult your campus placement service or the reference department of the main library.

Q How do I make a good impression during the job interview?

A Let's assume your résumé and letter of application clicked with a prospective employer and that you have been invited to an interview. How do you make the most of this important meeting?

First of all, do your homework. Find out all you can about the company— its products or services, the kinds of jobs it offers, what's happening in the industry as a whole, what's happening with this particular organization. Employers are pleased when you show you have taken the trouble to become familiar with their business—and frequently displeased when they discover you haven't bothered.

Next, you should get your thoughts together and try to anticipate some of the questions that are most likely to come up. Here are some of the more typical questions: Where do you hope to be in five years? Ten years? Why should we hire you? What can you do for us? What are your biggest strengths? Weaknesses? Why do you want to work for us? What has been your most enjoyable experience in college? Hoping to put you at ease, some interviewers will begin by asking you simply to talk about yourself. In any event, you need to think about your qualifications and about the type of job you are seeking, and why.

Dress neatly and conservatively. It's a good idea to avoid being either too formal or too casual. And when it comes to the interview itself:

- Be pleasant and friendly, but businesslike. (Note well: A good, firm handshake helps.)
- Let the employer control the discussion. Your answers should be complete, but brief. Don't ramble, and avoid dogmatic statements. And don't interrupt—even if you're itching to do so; positions are lost when courtesy and tact are missing in the interview.
- Stress your qualifications without exaggerating. The employer's questions will indicate the type of person wanted. Pick up on these cues and present your credentials accordingly. For example, if you're being interviewed for a management trainee position and the employer mentions that the job might require some contact with customers, respond by mentioning any experiences or courses that have prepared you to deal with people.
- In discussing your previous jobs, courses, or other experiences, avoid criticizing former employers, professors, or fellow students.
- Don't discuss your personal, domestic, or financial problems unless you are specifically asked about them.
- Use the interview to ask questions as well as answer them. Find out what the position involves, what opportunities for advancement may be open to you now or in the future, and anything else you can about the job.
- If the employer does not definitely offer you a job or indicate when you will hear about it, ask when you may call to learn the decision.
- Thank the employer for talking with you.

It's a good idea to rehearse beforehand. Have a friend pose questions to you and criticize your responses. Some college placement offices offer free TV camera and studio facilities so you can videotape yourself in a practice job interview. You can play back the tape in private and plan ways to improve.

Good guidebooks for successful job interviewing are available in all college libraries and most bookstores. One excellent source, from which many of the above guidelines were drawn, is a U.S. Department of Labor booklet, *Merchandising Your Job Talents.* You can write for it from the Labor Employment and Training Administration, Washington, D.C. 20213.

Q What are the pros and cons of summer school?

A The most obvious advantage of summer school is that it gives you the chance to pick up additional courses or to repeat courses you didn't do well in the first time. Summer school can help you get back on schedule or even ahead of schedule (if you want to try to graduate early).

Some students use summer school to concentrate on a really tough subject they don't want to tackle amid all the distractions of the regular academic year (organic chemistry is a popular choice in this category). If you hit the books hard during the summer term—there isn't much else to do on campus then but study anyhow—you might fatten up your GPA. Many hard-pressed students who have been slapped on academic probation use the summer session to scramble back into good standing.

For those who are more adventurous, the summer session can be ideal for exploring new territory. Admission is kept relatively open and simple. You might enroll for the summer at an Ivy League school, for example, or at a campus in a different and exotic part of the country.

Now for some disadvantages: Summer school costs money, and you could use the summer to work and save for next year. The campus is quieter (that is, duller) and hotter, and some dorms and classroom buildings won't be air conditioned. Also, many top professors jealously reserve their summers for research purposes, so the teachers in summer school may not always be the top of the line. Finally, there is the burnout factor. Going to college on a year-round basis can get to be a real drag; a hot, boring, fatiguing summer school may leave you in a rotten mood to begin the fall term.

There are many different summer session options. At the University of Mississippi, for example, students may attend one or two 6-week summer terms, while at the University of Kentucky there is one 4-week and one 8-week session. Cornell summer students can choose from courses offered during 3-week, 6-week, and 8-week sessions, along with dozens of special programs of varied lengths. Given all these possibilities, you may be able to attend summer school and get in some vacation or job time as well.

One note of caution: It's often necessary to prearrange for a transfer of summer school credit from one college to another, especially when it involves a course in your major, so clear your plans ahead of time with your faculty adviser.

Many students actually find the summer school refreshing. The learning environment is different. Classes are small, they meet every day, and good relations between student and teacher are possible. Your professors are relaxed, accessible, and almost always in a good mood. During summer school there is no committee work for faculty members, and those who teach get extra pay. So while summer school may or may not be for you, your prof probably likes it fine.

Q What are the pros and cons of correspondence courses?

A If you need an extra course or two, and summer school isn't convenient or affordable, then correspondence study might be the answer. You can enroll in correspondence courses at almost any time, even while you're taking classes in residence, though you'll need to get your dean's approval. For most correspondence courses, you receive a study guide and a reading list. You work through the written assignments at your own pace (there are usually about twenty-four assignments for a 3-credit course) and you then mail them in—one or two at a time—to an instructor who grades them and returns them to you. When you've done all your assignments, your teacher will arrange for your final examination to be administered near your home by a local school official.

Your college or university may have its own correspondence study office. If it doesn't, someone on your campus (begin with your academic dean) will have access to *The Independent Study Catalog,* which lists the thousands of courses offered by member schools of the National University Continuing Education Association. With the help of this guide, you should be able to locate the specific correspondence course you need.

Correspondence courses administered by colleges and universities cost between $25 and $75 per credit hour. Home-study courses sold by commercial correspondence schools may be far more expensive. An estimated 3 million Americans are believed to be enrolled in some form of correspondence instruction at present. Most are in vocational home-study programs, but nearly 250,000 are college students pursuing academic subjects.

Correspondence study does have its drawbacks. There's no classroom environment, no direct contact with a teacher, no discussion, no fixed schedule, no fellow students nearby for support. Each lesson may require 3 hours or more to finish, and the entire responsibility rests on your shoulders.

Many students start correspondence courses, but only disciplined, self-motivated individuals actually see them through to completion.

Despite the obvious difficulties, however, correspondence instruction continues to gain in popularity among today's college students. The low cost, flexibility, and convenience of correspondence courses make them well worth considering.

Q How private will my records be? Who is entitled to see my student file?

A Thanks to a series of privacy laws enacted during the past several years, only a very few individuals have access to your student files. In general, the list begins and ends with you and a handful of college personnel with legitimate educational interests in you, notably your faculty adviser and your dean.

There may even be some records in your files you yourself may not be permitted to see: confidential diagnoses issued by a physician or psychologist, for example, or some sensitive information provided by your secondary school. The other materials in your files, however, should be open to you, and you have the right to challenge any record you believe is inaccurate or misleading, such as a mistake on your grade transcript or an erroneous announcement that you were once placed on academic probation. These things happen.

Your files, which may be kept in various offices throughout the campus, contain a great deal of information, including your grades, fee payment records, faculty adviser's notations, entrance test scores, any financial aid requests and supporting data you've provided, letters of recommendation, and other related documents. The college must maintain this information, of course, but there's no need for you to worry that a prospective employer, or your nosy Aunt Minnie, will go snooping into your files. The laws are very clear on this score.

Q What advice do you have for prospective transfer students?

A Transferring from one school to another is far more common now than it once was. My own university, for example, enrolled 1,377 transfer students in a recent fall semester. One young man in a class of mine is currently attending his fourth college, and he is only a sophomore. (And at the rate he is spinning his wheels, he may remain a sophomore for some time.) Some transfers work out brilliantly; others leave students disappointed. All transfers, however, improve with adjustment and planning. Here are a few suggestions that may help:

- Become thoroughly familiar with the degree requirements at the new college through careful study of the catalog, visits to admissions people, and so on. Your present academic requirements become irrelevant when you transfer, and only your new institution's requirements apply. If the college you're planning to transfer to requires you to complete four semesters of a foreign language, for instance, then you might want to work on that requirement now, even if your present school doesn't require a foreign language.
- Don't be surprised if you lose some credits when you transfer. Not all courses are automatically accepted for credit by every college. You'll go through a transcript evaluation when you arrive at your new campus (it might be done by mail beforehand), and an admissions officer will tell you which courses are transferable and which aren't. Most degree programs are flexible enough to allow a considerable number of credits to be counted as electives. If you're lucky, you won't lose much by transferring, although you may find that the transferred credits will sharply reduce the number of elective credits you'll have for the future. As a general rule, basic courses such as Freshman English, Biology I, and so on are acknowledged much more readily than frothy electives such as Basket Weaving or Student Publications Practicum. And remedial courses probably won't transfer at all.
- Expect some scheduling problems when you arrive on your new campus. By the time you enroll for classes at the beginning of the semester, most students will have preregistered months before, which means they are far more likely to have been given their choices of professors, courses, class times, and the like. Many class sections will have been closed before the transfers arrive, and the pickings can be pretty slim.
- If you have a choice, transfer in for the fall semester, if only for social reasons. It's easier to adjust and make new friends in the fall when many other people—freshmen and transfers—are new to the campus as well.
- Don't panic if your grades slip a bit during your first semester at your new school. This is normal and should be chalked up to adjusting to a new grading system and a new environment. Most transfers recover nicely after one term. One experienced admissions officer, a man who

has examined literally thousands of student records over the years, tells me that the final grade point averages of transfer students—on his campus, at least—are virtually indistinguishable at graduation from those of students who had been at the same school for four years

- Finally, and most important, make certain that if you do transfer it's for the right reason. One student of mine actually transferred to a university in another state because she felt overworked as activities director of her sorority! As she was advised at the time, it would have been far easier on her, and probably on her family, if she had simply backed off from the sorority instead! By and large, colleges are more alike than they are different, and if you can't stand the professors or the students at College A you probably will encounter many of the same frustrations at College B.

Remember: The procedure is called Transfer—not Escape. Obviously there are worthy reasons for transferring—the strength of the academic program at the new college, financial considerations, and many more. These may outweigh the difficulties and time loss your transfer will require. Just be sure to examine your motives honestly and carefully before you make the move.

Q I don't know how high the college I'm planning to attend is rated nationally. What are the top colleges and universities?

A This question seems almost an obsession with some students, and with some parents. I understand their concern; an undergraduate education, for those fortunate enough to have a chance at one, comes only once in a lifetime. It represents an enormous expenditure of time and money, and obviously one should make every attempt to ensure that the investment is a wise one. But higher education is so fraught with variables and intangibles that any comparative ranking of schools is a risky gamble at best.

To begin with, few institutions are uniformly good or uniformly poor throughout their various academic and professional departments. Indiana University, for instance, has a superlative reputation in music, just as the University of Missouri is noted for its School of Journalism. Photography is considered an important strength at such schools as East Texas State and Western Kentucky University. This doesn't mean that the other departments at those universities are weak—far from it. But precious few institutions are wealthy enough, or lucky enough, to develop a powerhouse faculty in every single field of study. So when somebody asks me which are the best schools, my first response is another question: "Best at *what?*"

Even then we're on shaky ground. Some studies have been conducted in which college presidents or faculty members across the country were asked to list the best colleges or most distinguished departments. But what does "distinguished" actually mean? In this case, to a large extent, it means distinguished in terms of published research. Let me assure you that a professor's glittering reputation as a research scholar does not by any means guarantee that he or she is at the same time a good teacher. Some of the country's outstanding researchers prove to be absolute disasters in the classroom, particularly when the classroom is filled with undergraduate students. Indeed, some of the more awkward moments I faced during my years as an administrator came in smoothing over communications problems between a brilliant scholar on our faculty and his students. A professor can have a well-deserved international reputation for research and yet at the same time be embarrassingly incoherent when trying to explain his or her theories to young people in classes.

Also, there's no assurance that the distinguished faculty members will even be accessible to you. You might enroll at a famous university in order to study with Professor X—only to learn that Professor X has (1) disappeared from the country on an extended sabbatical leave, (2) become a full-time consultant or dean, or (3) reduced his or her teaching load to one or two advanced seminars open only to graduate students.

None of this is to detract from the world-class faculties at the best-known colleges. My point is that there are fine teachers on most campuses—even on those campuses that do not boast strong reputations for scholarly research. A great many students have become academic misfits in their attempts to satisfy somebody else's notions about the value of getting a degree from one of the "top schools in the country."

In other words, the "top" college for you is the one where you feel most comfortable and where you are challenged to do your best work. It's as simple—and as complicated—as that.

AND, FINALLY...

Several years ago, some professors and staff people at one university where I worked wrote a report on the freshman year. It was a massive study of how one institution handled its freshmen—and how the freshmen handled themselves—and it contained this thoughtful passage:

> This (the freshman year) is the time for exploration, skill-building, sight-setting, reaching for that stable balance between dependence and independence. It is the time for putting first things first.
>
> Or it is the time for none of these. It can be the time of following whim and fad and printed directions. It can be the time of drawing false conclusions because of unexamined certainties about truth, self, and the future. It can be the time of getting by with undeveloped skills, of continuing school with grade thirteen. It can be a time when being oneself means simply continuing to be only what one was always expected to be. The consequence in this case is the postponement of the freshman year until the sophomore year, or later, or never.

The freshman year, like the entire college experience, isn't necessarily a crossroads—no matter what the orientation speakers may tell you; some students have a wretched time of it as undergraduates, then go on to lead perfectly wonderful lives afterward. But the freshman year does, in fact, usually present the greatest set of challenges to you. If there are big, intelligent commitments of time and energy at the beginning, there will most likely be terrific payoffs later on.

You'll probably enjoy college. Most students do. I've been teaching freshmen, and learning from them, for nearly twenty-five years now. And despite what you may have heard about troubled youth, the selfish "Me" generation, and similar alarmist appraisals, the freshmen I've observed tend to be open, friendly, generous, upbeat young men and women who are happy about who they are and where they are. Marya Mannes could have been thinking of them when she declared: "What I have will do; what I make of it is up to me."

What you've got is, or can be, plenty. Here's hoping college helps you make the most of it, and that you have a marvelous time along the way.